T0206540

JOY IN
TIGERTOWN

JOY IN
TIGERTOWN

*A Determined Team, a Resilient City, and
Our Magical Run to the 1968 World Series*

MICKEY LOLICH *with* **TOM GAGE**

TRIUMPH
BOOKS

Library of Congress Cataloging-in-Publication Data

Names: Gage, Tom | Lolich, Mickey.
Title: Joy in Tigertown : a determined team, a resilient city, and our magical run to the 1968 world series / Tom Gage, Mickey Lolich ; foreword by Jim Leyland.
Description: Chicago, Illinois : Triumph Books, 2018.
Identifiers: LCCN 2017061561 | ISBN 9781629375830 (paperback)
Subjects: LCSH: Detroit Tigers (Baseball team)—History. | World Series (Baseball) (1968) | BISAC: SPORTS & RECREATION / Baseball / General. | TRAVEL / United States / Midwest / East North Central (IL, IN, MI, OH, WI).
Classification: LCC GV875.D6 G35 2018 | DDC 796.357/640977434—dc23 LC record available at https://lccn.loc.gov/2017061561

This book is available in quantity at special discounts for your group or organization. For further information, contact:

Triumph Books LLC
814 North Franklin Street
Chicago, Illinois 60610
(312) 337-0747
www.triumphbooks.com

Printed in U.S.A.
ISBN: 978-1-62937-583-0
Design by Meghan Grammer

To my wonderful family
and to the baseball fans of Detroit—
for their love of the game
—Mickey Lolich

To my wife, Lisa,
for her love, her assistance,
and her courage
—Tom Gage

"There'll be Joy in Tigertown.
We'll sing you a song,
when the Bengals bring the pennant home
where it belongs."

Contents

Foreword

I remember when I traveled to Lakeland, where the Tigers train in Florida during the spring, for the first time. After graduating from high school, I signed as a catcher with Detroit in 1963, and when my parents put me on the bus to head south—my mom crying as she waved good-bye—it was the start of the biggest adventure of my life.

I hadn't been to many places up to that point, but here I was going to spring training as a player in the Detroit Tigers' organization. I couldn't have been happier—or more excited. I took one of those sleek, double-deck Greyhound buses all the way from Toledo, Ohio, to Lakeland. They were called Scenicruisers, and a seat upstairs in the back gave you a great view of everything you rode past.

When we arrived in Lakeland, but before we got to the station, the bus drove past Henley Field, where I could see ballplayers working out. Henley Field was where the Tigers trained and played their spring games before Joker Marchant Stadium was built. Trying to get the best view I could, I remember thinking the guys who were working out that day might be big league ballplayers. That made a huge impression on me. It could have been Al Kaline taking some swings. It could have been Bill Freehan catching a young pitcher, Norm Cash hitting one over the fence in right during batting practice, or Dick McAuliffe fielding grounders.

That quick drive-by was my introduction to Lakeland and my welcome to professional baseball. I don't care which of the two you call it. But it really sank in when I saw those guys that I was actually at spring training with the Tigers, the team my Aunt Inez took me to see as a kid at Briggs Stadium.

I didn't know how long my time as a so-called prospect was going to last, especially since I had a couple of All-American catchers as roommates in the minor leagues—and I was just a scrawny kid from Perrysburg High School. But I was going to give it everything I had.

I figured the players on the field that day at Henley were many of the guys I looked up to. I just wanted to do what they already had done and to someday, somehow get to the big leagues. But I never made it as a player. I never made it above the Double A level, in fact—and I once said that I'd give up everything else that I achieved in my career to have spent one day in the majors as a player.

I always had tremendous respect for players like Freehan, Cash, Kaline, and Mickey Lolich. When I would come over from the minor league complex to help as an extra catcher at big league camp, they could not have been nicer to me. But that's all I ever did. I helped out. When I would catch Lolich, it was never in a game. It was always on the side.

A few years ago when I was managing the Tigers, Mickey came to Lakeland to throw out the ceremonial first pitch before an exhibition game. I was honored when he asked me to be his catcher. "After all those times I warmed you up, I finally get to catch you between the lines," I told him. When he signed the ball, saying how happy he was about how my career turned out, it was an emotional moment for me.

As for other Tigers of that era, I can say that as a catcher it was always special to see Freehan go about his work. And I'm proud to say that Kaline and Willie Horton have become longtime friends of mine.

I wasn't a Tiger in 1968. I'm not writing this foreword to pretend I was. I'm writing it because I respected the players who were. I admired what they overcame to take the 1967 season to the last day. I admired that they won one of the greatest World Series ever in 1968—and that many of them are among the greatest names in Tigers history.

They didn't have to treat me as well as they did whenever I was around them. I was just a kid hoping against hope to make it to the majors. Years later, I'm still grateful that I learned something from them along the way. And this is part of what I learned: I will always appreciate my years with the

Tigers—then or now, past or present—in the majors as a manager or in the minors as a player and manager. They've always felt like family to me.

So congratulations on your book and your great career, Mickey. But above all, thanks for being you.

—**Jim Leyland**
Detroit Tigers manager, 2006–13

Introduction

I haven't always wanted to write a book. But ever since I've had grandchildren, I have wanted to. They've known Grandpa played baseball. They've known I was a Detroit Tiger and that I pitched in the World Series. But they haven't known what it was really like for me to be a big league ballplayer. Or what it took along the way for me to get to the majors.

My children, of course, grew up with me playing the game and also with me being away from home because of the game. Among my favorite photos is the one that appeared in the Detroit papers of Kimberly, my oldest daughter, giving Daddy a kiss after we won Game 5.

But it's not just my story my grandchildren will read about. I want them to know how the Tigers helped repair the city of Detroit after the riots. Detroit was reeling. People needed something to feel good about. They also needed to feel good together. We came close but didn't give them a championship to cheer about in 1967 and we felt badly about that. But we came back in 1968 determined to put a smile back on the city's face. We knew early in spring training that we had a good team, one that could win it all. It was a dream come true for all of us, fans and players alike, when we indeed won it all.

Winning three games in the World Series isn't all that I accomplished as a big leaguer. I'm proud of the fact that I pitched more than 300 innings four seasons in a row. I'm proud that I was durable and that my team could rely on me. I'm proud that when I retired I had the most strikeouts of any left-hander who ever pitched. I'm also proud that from a kid, who didn't know anything about the game while growing up—not even the difference between a ball and a strike—I became a major league pitcher.

Keep in mind the only items I ever threw before I was 12 years old were rocks at a nearby creek and the figs that fell from my grandfather's tree. My grandparents, Mijo and Lucy, were from Croatia. My grandmother never spoke a word of English. They lived four doors down from us in Portland. My father, Steve, never pushed me to play baseball because he didn't understand the game. To help make ends meet, my mother, Marge, worked for a lumber company and before that as a waitress. They were good, hard-working people.

And after I made it to the majors, I found myself in the Air National Guard on duty to defend Detroit from the lawlessness that threatened it in 1967.

So I do have a story to tell and, with the help of Tom Gage, I'm telling it. Enjoy the journey.

Chapter 1

The Riots

"They're killing people. They're burning down the town."
—outfielder Jim Northrup

The bus pulled up with several prisoners—violent men from the streets who'd been causing trouble—on it. I didn't see the individual who made the bloody attempt, but I heard about it. He broke the window next to his seat on the bus and tried to slit his throat on the jagged glass. I never found out how badly he injured himself. Or if he even survived. Such were the riots of 1967 in Detroit, though.

They took a toll not only on the city, or on the victims of the violence, but also on those distraught enough to take to the streets. Detroit wouldn't recover from the destruction for years. Maybe decades. Or possibly it still hasn't. Within hours, though, the riots had ruined some lives and changed others.

One day I was a pitcher; the next day I was on active duty for the Air National Guard.

One day I had a baseball in my hand; the next day I had a rifle slung over my shoulder. One day Detroit wasn't in the national news. The next day—with its fires, its looting, and its killing—it had *become* the national news. As president Lyndon Johnson said, "Law and order have broken down in Detroit, Michigan."

I'm not going to tell you I was assigned to the middle of the mayhem—because I wasn't. I neither fired my weapon at anyone, nor was I fired upon. I'm also not going to tell you I was ever at the epicenter of the unrest. But until peace was restored, we didn't know what we would or would not experience. Until we returned to our civilian jobs, we were soldiers following orders. Until I was Mickey Lolich, left-handed pitcher again, I was Mickey Lolich, sergeant.

In the same city where we worked, we also served. In the same city where we made our living, lives were lost. On July 23, 1967, a hot summer Sunday, there was smoke out there somewhere beyond left field at Tiger Stadium. We couldn't tell how near it was. We couldn't tell how far—but as usual, where there was smoke, there was fire.

Plenty of it.

Detroit was beginning to burn. Indeed it was.

When the trouble began, though, it seemed like such a normal day. Not that I want to say it was normal for me to lose a baseball game, but that's what I had just done—I'd lost the first game of a doubleheader at Tiger Stadium 4–2 to the New York Yankees. The game had pissed me off because it was more of the same for me. I hadn't been pitching very well, which is a way of saying I was 5–12 with a 4.40 ERA after taking the loss. We had a pretty good team at nine games over .500, but my record was horseshit. The loss was my 10th in a row. My season was spinning out of control. "Be careful, Mickey," the stadium guard told me when I left before the second game of the doubleheader was over. "Something bad is going on out there."

That's what I had heard. But I would see none of it. My way home took me away from the smoke, not toward it. I didn't know the extent of the problem until much later. On the broadcast for the second game, the announcers weren't saying anything about it either. General manager Jim Campbell didn't want to alarm the fans. No one did. So the nightcap was played as if it was just another Sunday. We won the game for a split. It was John Hiller's first major league victory.

But my teammates were told after the last out of the second game that their safety could not be guaranteed. Many of them drove home through clouds of smoke. Meanwhile, the blaze beyond left field—out on nearby 12th Street as we would learn later—kept growing. Violence was erupting everywhere. Willie Horton said he drove to one of the trouble spots and pleaded from atop his car with those in the streets to calm down. He failed.

They told him to drive away, that they didn't want him to get hurt. Not even the immensely popular Horton, the first African American baseball star in Detroit—a son of the city— could make the looters listen. The riots were spreading.

What had triggered the exploding unrest was an earlier altercation that took place when police raided a Detroit bar serving liquor after hours without a license to do so—a blind pig, in other words.

More than 80 people were arrested. But as those initially charged were waiting to be transferred to a police station, a bottle was thrown at a police van. One thing led to another, including the looting of a nearby store, and the violence escalated from there.

Soon it was more than unrest. It was a full-fledged riot, one of the worst any city had ever experienced. By the time it ended on its fifth day, 43 people had been killed. It didn't matter much, given far more serious circumstances, but we had baseball games to play and we couldn't play them that week at Tiger Stadium, which wasn't far from the center of the trouble.

So, over the objection of some players who wanted to stay home and make sure their families were safe—"They're killing people out there," said outfielder Jim Northrup. "They're burning down the town"—the next series was moved to Baltimore. We were to fly out the following morning, Monday the 24th. Thinking I was leaving town, I drove to Tiger Stadium the next day to board the team bus to the airport. But just after I arrived, one of the ballpark guards said I had a phone call. It was Sgt. Zenker of the Air National Guard saying my unit, the 191st Combat Support Squadron, had been activated.

When I asked what that meant, he said it meant I needed to report to the base at Metropolitan Airport as fast as I could. So instead of going to Baltimore with the team, I was soon heading back home to get into my "other" uniform and then joining my unit. From there we didn't know where we were going. But it wouldn't take long to find out.

I'd been in the Air National Guard since 1963 and would stay in it until 1969. I had an annual commitment to attend the guard's summer camp in Alpena, Michigan, for two weeks, but if I had a scheduled start during those two weeks, I could fly down to make it. It wasn't easy to get ready for those starts. I'd try to throw during the camp, but I had a difficult time finding catchers who could actually catch me. I didn't want to hurt anyone by throwing with major league velocity. So I've had people suggest to me that dividing my summer for years like that cost me more than 20 wins throughout my career. But I don't make a big deal about that. It's not a complaint and never will be. I did the best I could in both uniforms.

We had already been to camp, though, when the 1967 riots began. They started on a Sunday, and we were activated as a unit for 10 days, starting Monday. The first thing we did after reporting to the base was to board a bus that would take us to a radio tower we were supposed to guard. I don't know where the hell I was at, but I was a sergeant in command of 11 other guys. The tower was on the roof of a Detroit Public Works building, but all I could see around me were garbage trucks. "Is that what we're doing, guarding garbage trucks?" I asked another officer. He grinned and then explained to me that up on the roof was the tower we were assigned to guard. That's what we did the first night.

But all we were given to eat were some K rations from the Korean War that we didn't like the looks of. They were nasty. So my first order was to tell everyone to cough up $5, and we'd somehow find something to eat. The guys in the unit said $5 wouldn't cover it, so they gave me $10 instead. We sent a volunteer to a takeout spot about three blocks away. But he had to be protected, so there I was walking down the street, wearing a helmet and fatigues while carrying an M-1. That's how we walked into the restaurant. Everyone turned around, saw me with the rifle, and their eyes grew as big as can be. A soldier off the street, carrying a rifle, picking up a carryout order? It doesn't happen every day.

Well, we picked up our 12 cheeseburgers, 12 milkshakes, and 12 orders of fries and took them back. But before we did, the owner came out and asked what was going on, so we told him we were guarding the radio tower down the street. "I guess that's good in case there's trouble that breaks out around here," he said. "This order is on me." He didn't recognize me for being a major league pitcher, which was fine with me. He was just happy our unit was close if the violence spread.

But shortly after that, we were pulled out of our initial location. They had checked the records and discovered that I was the second highest qualifier in my guard unit as far as being accurate with a rifle. That presented a couple of problems. The first was that they didn't want anyone shooting at me, but the second was that they didn't want me shooting back. So they assigned me to the motor pool as a driver for the major who was in charge of the troops downtown.

The Beaubien Street police station was command head-quarters, but it was the safest place in the world with machine guns all around it. Plus we didn't have any more food problems because the wives of all the police officers stationed there kept sending them meals. When my major wanted to move, he'd let me know. But I was free to wander otherwise. I saw a lot down there at the station I never want to see again—like I saw prisoners sitting on the floor of the garage, and to help with overflow, they sent for 10 Detroit city buses. But for security reasons, only two guys at a time were allowed to use the Porta-Johns—or as we said in the military, the latrine. That led to prisoners using the buses as their bathroom, which meant—I heard later—that those buses could never be used again. I mean the stench was something else. So they had to be burned.

Still on active status, I was allowed to go home that night, but the possibility of joining the team in Baltimore was out of the question. From there, though, the Tigers had three more cities to go to. Lasting two weeks, it turned into a 13-game road trip that included yet another stop in Baltimore. But with a 7–6 record, it became neither a maker nor a breaker of the 1967 season. We were in fourth place, three games out of first when the trip began and in fourth place, three games out when it ended.

I went nearly three weeks without pitching—from the doubleheader start that I lost on July 23, the day the riots began, to August 11 in the second game of another doubleheader. It was incredibly strange, however, that my season reversed itself when I resumed pitching. I went from a 0–10 slump to a 9–1 streak. I also went from an ERA of 5.09 during the slump to a 1.33 ERA after I returned to pitching. Amazing.

But suddenly we were in the middle of a pennant race that only made the city sadder and the fans madder when we came up short on the final day of the season. "From total excitement, boom, it was over," I said at the time. "I've never seen so many grown men cry in all my life," Gates Brown said on HBO's *A City on Fire* documentary.

The riots were devastating to the city of Detroit. They lasted five days. According to reports, in addition to the 43 people who were killed, nearly 1,200 were injured. More than 4,600 looters were among the 7,000 people arrested. More than 2,500 stores were looted or burned. Another 400 buildings had to be demolished because of extensive damage. Nearly 400 families were rendered homeless or displaced. And I—while not even coming close to where it was worst—will never forget my small role.

We remained active but on call for another week. It was the only time while I was in the Michigan Air National Guard that our squadron was activated. The rest of the time, years of it, was pretty routine. Because I was part of the motor pool, I would drive pilots from their quarters to their planes. I'd pick them up in a truck, take them out to their aircraft, and then I'd wait for them to return. There was a lot of waiting when I rather would have been with the team. I was the only Tigers' ballplayer on the base, so most people knew who I was and what my civilian job was. That meant a lot of baseball talk. I once was assigned to pick up an arriving general, who proceeded to sit on the hood of my car and just wanted to talk baseball.

I made some friends in the guard. But when my obligation was up, I can't say I minded. Probably my most memorable moments had involved two phone calls. One was the call I got at the ballpark from Sgt. Zenker, my commanding officer for the entire time I was in the guard, to inform me we'd been activated. I'd tell you his first name, but, to be honest, I'm not sure of it. I just called him Sarge. With his call, though, I realized just how big the riots were becoming.

But to match the impact of getting that first call was the one I received days later to tell me the riots were finally over. "We're no longer active," Sarge told me in that second call. "Now you can go play baseball again."

So I did.

Chapter 2

1967

"So close, so close."
—outfielder Willie Horton

To fully understand the joy of 1968 in Detroit, following what the city suffered through the year before, it is essential to understand the end of the Tigers' 1967 season. In the same year that the riots took their toll, we could have made Detroit smile again by winning the American League pennant. And for much of the season's final week, it looked like we were going to do exactly that.

But with two days remaining, the question of how it would end remained agonizingly unanswered. It had been a turbulent season for many Tigers, including me. Sometimes I think "especially me," but it would be selfish to think so. I did lose 10 in a row, though—a slump of such personal impact that it made me wonder if I would be able to adequately provide for my family. "I tell you, I've awakened more than once during the night and started thinking about things," I confided to

Detroit Free Press columnist Joe Falls that summer. "I mean, you get to thinking about your career, the way it should be going—and then something like this happens, losing all these games in a row. The thing is I took a salary cut this year. I won 14 games last season but took a cut. It makes you think, if that's the case, what are they going to do to me next season?"

I was worried about my future. That was plain to see. But I couldn't trace my slump to anything I was doing wrong on the mound. "What gets me," I said in that same conversation with Falls, "is that I've been pitching the same way as when I won 18 games two years ago. My fastball is moving the same way. My curve is breaking the same way. I'm hitting the corners. I'm locating the ball around the knees. I'm jamming guys the way you should. But all I've done is lose."

My record was 5–2 when the nonstop slump began. The Tigers scored only five runs in my next five starts. Only once during the drought did we score more than two runs while I was on the mound, and that happened in the worst game I had all year—an 11–5 loss to the Minnesota Twins, in which I didn't get out of the third inning. That defeat was my sixth in a row, and unbeknownst to me, I had four more to go before I finally won a game. I lost the four by scores of 2–0, 3–2, 3–2, and 4–2. Suffice it to say, it was a trying time.

It was a stretch that could easily ruin a season for a starting pitcher—and also for the pitcher's team because the slump was an extended one. From May 20 through August 10, I didn't win a game. I was 0–10. Worse was the feeling of letting my team down because the Tigers were 0–11 with me pitching during that time.

It was a nightmare.

In fact, the day I lost my 10th in a row, I was driving home from the ballpark a little too fast—or maybe a lot too fast. And sure enough, I got pulled over for speeding. When the officer asked for my driver's license, he recognized my name. "Michael Lolich," he said. "Is that you, Mickey?"

When I said it was, he replied, "Go on home. You have enough problems."

Despite my individual losing streak, the team had an overall 40–42 record. Better yet, we lost only two games in the standings. We were in second place, a half game out of first at the beginning of it and in fourth just two-and-a-half games out when I finally started winning again.

And, thankfully, I did start winning again. In my last 10 starts of 1967, I went 8–1 with four shutouts and a 1.26 ERA. But more importantly the Tigers went 9–1. I bounced back—we did, too—and suddenly the season was fun again. Go figure, though. I wasn't doing anything differently than when I was losing. At least that's how it felt to me. It was no time, however, to look back and wonder why. With 50 games remaining, we were in the middle of a pennant race.

And what a pennant race it turned out to be—especially after Labor Day. We went from fourth place to first with a win one day but sank from first to fourth with a loss another day. That's the kind of wild ride it was. There were four teams—us, the Boston Red Sox, the Twins, and the Chicago White Sox—scrambling for first place the entire month of September.

At one point or other, each of the four was in sole possession of first. Back and forth it went. It looked like the Twins might take charge. Then it looked like we would. Then it was Boston's turn. The White Sox had the toughest road but weren't backing off. When the final week of the regular season began, they were only a game out of first. At that point the White Sox were in a better position than we were. With a week left, we were in fourth, one-and-a-half games out, coming off a heartbreaking loss to the Washington Senators.

Through the eighth inning of that game, the Senators had been held to two runs on three hits by the combination of Joe Sparma and Fred Lasher. Going into the bottom of the ninth, we led 4–2. The Red Sox, Twins, and White Sox would all win their games that day. We needed to keep pace by holding onto our two-run lead against the Senators, who were playing for nothing but pride. Never underestimate pride as a motivating factor, however. With that funky delivery of his, Lasher had retired the side in order in the eighth inning. There was no reason to believe he wouldn't get through the ninth as well.

But baseball is always baseball. Anything can happen at any time. Once again, that point was proven. On a slow grounder to second base in the bottom of the ninth—with Mike Epstein of the Senators on first and no outs—Tigers infielder Dick McAuliffe made the mistake of trying to tag the runner instead of simply throwing the ball to first for the sure out. Mac slipped after failing to tag Epstein, giving the batter, Frank Coggins, enough time to beat his throw to first. "I was trying to get a double play," McAuliffe said. But instead, the Senators had the tying run on base in the ninth with no outs. They took advantage of the opportunity with a three-run inning capped by Fred Valentine's game-winning single on a 0–2 pitch from John Hiller.

It was a crushing loss, no matter how much we tried to brush away our disappointment. We'd blown a two-run lead in the ninth to the Senators and with a week left we suddenly weren't looking like a team capable of winning the pennant. "We can lose one more, but that's it," manager Mayo Smith said after the game.

I agreed with Mayo about our chances. We were making it more difficult on ourselves than it had to be. In four of our last five defeats, we'd blown ninth-inning leads. The dream of giving Detroit something to celebrate after its tragic summer wasn't gone. But it was getting more unlikely. So when the final week of the regular season began and the dust of our despair at D.C. Stadium had settled, the Twins led the Red Sox by a half game, the White Sox by one game, and us by one-and-a-half games.

Over in the National League, the St. Louis Cardinals were cruising. Leading the second-place San Francisco Giants by 11 ½ games, the Cardinals already knew they were headed to the World Series. Keep in mind that there were no divisional play-offs yet. The AL race was still up for grabs, however, and would be all week.

On Monday we lost 2–0 to the New York Yankees, but the Twins also lost. Al Downing blanked us on four hits, dropping Earl Wilson's record to 22–11. After that, we faced the rest of the week without knowing if Wilson—our ace that year—would get another chance to be a factor. We had five games left but still trailed by one-and-a-half games.

On Tuesday, I overcame a throwing error I made to blank the Yankees 1–0 at Yankee Stadium. As an example of just how crazy baseball can be, this victory was the seventh in my last eight decisions—after I'd lost 10 in a row. The shutout was my second in a row. Mayo told reporters after the game, "Mickey is a better pitcher now than he's ever been."

As I said, I was getting vastly better results with the same stuff. That Yankees game was a strange one even so. For instance, catcher Bill Freehan was ejected for throwing his mask too closely to umpire Hank Soar's feet while arguing that a passed ball had been a foul ball. It didn't look like anything Bill should have gotten thrown out for, and his absence left a void, but we rolled with it. The victory didn't get us closer to first place, however, because the Twins also won. As *Free Press* writer George Cantor put it, we still had a pulse, but it was weak.

Wednesday proved to be a hugely important day for us, even though it was a rare midweek off day. The Twins lost at home to the California Angels, and the White Sox were all but knocked out of it by losing two to the A's in Kansas City. With four games left, we were a game out, but with two more games to play than either the Twins or Red Sox, we still knew we could afford only one more defeat at most.

We would have been the only contender to play on Thursday—had we played at all—but we were rained out at home against the Angels. So the incredibly tense pennant race became even more compressed than it had been. Because of the rainout, we were looking at playing four games in the next three days while the Red Sox and Twins had only two games remaining.

And yet that still would have been fine...if the weather had cooperated.

But it was wintry in Detroit on Friday, so our doubleheader was moved to Saturday, which meant that after being idle for three days (an off day followed by two bad weather days) we would finish the regular season with back-to-back double-headers. Meanwhile, the Twins would be playing in Boston with a chance to win it outright. By then, the only one of the four contenders out of it were the White Sox. Defending his underdog team, Sox manager Eddie Stanky took elimination hard. "Don't ask me who I think is going to win it," he said. "I don't care. All year long the elephants feared the mice. Well, they can have it all to themselves now. We're out of it. There's only one thing I really wanted, outside of winning it...I wanted to hang on until the final day and make everyone sweat until the last minute."

The White Sox had coaxed everything they could out of themselves. But it was our turn next to face the toughest road. On three days' rest, I pitched the opener against the Angels on Saturday. Fortunately, everything I'd had that had worked well for awhile worked well again. Scoring four runs in the first two innings, we won the game 5–0.

The shutout was my third in a row, but would it be enough to help get us into the World Series? Winning the second game of that Saturday doubleheader appeared essential. With a 6–2 lead against the Angels after seven innings of the nightcap, a sweep definitely looked possible.

But Lasher ran into trouble in the eighth when all four of the batters he faced got on base—three of them on singles, the other on a walk. When reliever Hank Aguirre came into the game, we led 6–4, but the Angels had runners at first and third with no outs.

Aguirre then made the mistake that later had him shaking his head in disbelief and Mayo muttering to himself. On Bubba Morton's tapper back to the mound, Hank didn't check Don Mincher, the runner at third. He let him score uncontested while opting to throw the ball to first base instead. "If he'd thrown Mincher out," Mayo moaned, "the inning would have been different."

Hank couldn't believe the mistake he had made. "I've made that play a thousand times," he told reporters after the game. "I should have looked at Mincher, but I didn't expect him to go. It was a dumb play by me, but it was also a dumb play for him to run. There were two dumb guys out there."

With our lead narrowed to a run, the Angels didn't back off. They took the lead later in the eighth on Jim Fregosi's two-run single off Hiller. Incredibly, we had fallen apart in the eighth and would lose the game 8–6. It was a hard defeat to take, but we didn't have the time to cry about it. We knew we still had a chance to extend the season on Sunday—a slim one but a chance. We needed to win both games. "No sense quitting now," Wilson said. "We've been fighting all year. We may as well keep on fighting."

In short, we needed to win both games on Sunday to force a Monday playoff against whichever team won the final game between Minnesota and Boston. With one day left, the three teams were separated by a half game. I was not available to start on Sunday because of Saturday's start. But I said I could help in relief if needed. We would know after the first game if we were still in it. If we won the opener, we would be. And we won the opener.

With a two-run home run from Willie Horton in the first inning and a costly outfield error by Roger Repoz in the third, we gave Sparma a 5–1 lead to work with after three innings. Still a thorn to us, Mincher hit a pair of home runs for the Angels, but we held on for a 6–4 decision. In the meantime, the Red Sox eliminated the Twins in Boston with a 5–3 victory.

The Twins held out hope until the ninth when Rod Carew— in the final at-bat of his rookie season—hit into a double play against Jim Lonborg after a leadoff single by Ted Uhlaender. Rich Rollins ended the game with a pop-up to short. The Red Sox were 92–70 at that point. We were 91–70. All the Sox could do—all anyone could do, for that matter—was to see how our second game against the Angels would turn out. If we won, there'd be a Monday playoff at Fenway Park to determine the pennant winner.

We had Denny McLain going for us in the Sunday nightcap. He'd had a good season, but after an excellent August in which he won five of seven starts, he'd been winless in September.

Not only that, but Denny hadn't pitched for nearly two weeks because of dislocated toes. When reporters told McLain there were those who didn't believe the story that his foot had fallen asleep while he dozed on the couch, Denny said, "I know. But what am I going to do: make up a story?" he told the *Free Press.* "It's too crazy to make up. My foot went to sleep, and I turned my toes when I got up. I know Mayo is sore at me, but what can I do? I got hurt."

There was also a *story* circulating that a raccoon outside a sliding door at his house had startled McLain into awkwardly landing on his toes, but Denny claimed that hadn't been the case. "It happened just like I said it did. Believe me, nobody feels more ridiculous than I do," McLain said. "I went down to the ballpark for some treatment, but I went early in the day so I wouldn't have to face the guys. If they'd seen me, I would have turned 212 different colors. Sure, it was a dumb injury, but I couldn't help it. I think I can still help the club, though. All I want is a chance to pitch."

In the final game of the regular season, with everything on the line, he got that chance. After the first two innings, we were feeling good. Thanks to a two-run home run by Jim Northrup and an RBI triple by McAuliffe, we led 3–1. But with the help of a home run from Mincher, the Angels stormed back to take a 4–3 lead in the third.

With Mayo going to his bullpen in the third, it was Hiller, not Denny, who gave up the home run to Mincher—and it was Mike Marshall who then allowed a two-run triple to Repoz in the Angels' three-run fourth. When Buck Rodgers singled in a run off Aguirre in the fifth, we trailed 8–3.

Lasher tossed two scoreless innings of relief, but at the plate, we hit into double plays in both the fifth and the sixth. With the season ticking down, there was no comeback in sight.

Hope arrived with McAuliffe's two-run single with two outs in the seventh. Instead of a five-run deficit, we now trailed by three runs. I was able to hold the Angels at bay by retiring the side in order in the ninth, so it all came down to our last at-bats.

We needed three runs to tie, four to win.

Freehan's leadoff double was a good start. Don Wert followed with a walk, which meant the tying run was at the plate with no outs—with me coming up to bat.

The game had been an official scorer's nightmare, of course. The Angels used five pitchers to our eight. Lenny Green was announced as a pinch-hitter for me after the walk to Wert—our fourth pinch-hitter of the game—but when the Angels replaced right-hander Minnie Rojas with lefty George Brunet, Jim Price hit for Green. Price's fly ball to shallow left was the first out of the inning. "I wanted to put the ball in play, which I did," Price said. "But I remember thinking I just missed it."

That brought up McAuliffe, who had driven in two runs in his previous at-bat and who also had tripled in a run in the second inning. With a hot bat, he was our best hope. Instead of another big hit, though, Mac topped a grounder to second baseman Bobby Knoop, who converted it into a game-ending 4-6-3 double play. And just like that in the darkening gloom of Tiger Stadium at 7:43 PM—with a plane waiting, if needed, to take the team to Boston—the 1967 season abruptly ended for us.

We finished tied for second place, a game behind the Red Sox. But the silence of being the runner-up was deafening. "So close, so close," Horton said. "We have nothing to be ashamed of. We gave it all we got," Al Kaline said.

Not only did we get over our disappointment quickly, we used it as a rallying cry all winter. Instead of it being a long offseason for us, the opposite turned out to be true. We felt we'd been shortchanged. We understood why we had to play back-to-back doubleheaders on the final weekend with the pennant on the line, but it had been a grueling challenge all the same.

We should have won, and it really bothered us that we didn't.

So we could hardly wait to get back out there the next spring because of how 1967 ended. If we moped at all, we didn't mope for long because we knew we were going to be good. And I remember a lot of players from other teams telling us the next spring that we were going to be good. Full of confidence, we sensed from the get-go that 1968 was going to be our year.

Chapter 3

Clinching the Pennant

"You might have saved the city."

—Tigers owner John Fetzer

Someone once asked me at what point in 1968 did I know we were going to win the American League pennant. In fact, I've been asked that question more than once over the years. But the answer is easy. I knew we'd win in '68 when we didn't win in '67.

We went home for the winter with such resolve, following that disappointment, that I was sure we'd come back in the spring and that it was going to be our year. I don't think we ever wavered in our confidence, even during our most grueling road trip of the season, which, I promise you, was a severe test. In August we lost five of six games on a trip to New York and Chicago—all by one run. We also played a 19-inning tie that had to be entirely made up two days later as the first game of a doubleheader against the New York Yankees.

Talk about a long day. John Hiller pitched nine innings of scoreless relief in that tie game, which was called because of a 1:00 AM curfew. Putting us in an even worse mood was the fact that at the beginning of the trip we lost Dick McAuliffe to a five-day suspension for charging the mound in a brawl involving Tommy John. Spinning our wheels the entire time while he was out, we definitely missed Mac. In the opener of the series at Yankee Stadium, Tom Tresh hit a two-run home run in the second inning from which we did not recover in a 2–1 loss.

With a runner on in the first inning of the second game, Roy White connected off of Denny McLain, and that, too, was enough to beat us. Mel Stottlemyre didn't strike anyone out yet somehow went the distance with a four-hitter. We lost the third game 6–5 when Pat Dobson blew a 5–1 lead in the sixth. And I didn't help matters by being terrible—I mean absolutely terrible—in the series finale, walking seven before exiting with no outs in the fourth. This is how bad I was: I allowed a leadoff single in the first inning, then walked three in a row. When I also walked the first two batters I faced in the fourth, including the pitcher, my day was done. We lost 5–4.

Making matters worse, we lost the last game of the trip 2–1 in Chicago when Luis Aparicio of the White Sox hit a two-out, walk-off single in the bottom of the ninth. This was the season's speed bump for us. We'd gone on the trip with a seven-and-a-half game lead over the Baltimore Orioles but came home with just a four-game edge. Not only that, we were suddenly losing close games.

Were we worried? I don't think so. But the Orioles were red hot. In their last 62 games, they'd gone 42–20 while we'd been 38–24. The Birds were steadily creeping closer. Getting home from Chicago, we were greeted by a *Detroit Free Press* headline saying "AL Lead Shrinks to 4." Alarms were being sounded. Fans were getting nervous.

It was gut check time for us, to be sure, and we responded like the champions we were destined to be. In the next 10 games, we were 8–2 while the suddenly stumbling Orioles went 3–7. Two one-run losses in a row at home to the last-place Washington Senators were setbacks for them, especially a blown three-run lead in the second game. Then they lost two of three to us in a series that was called their last gasp.

Just like that, we were up by nine games again. Instead of fretting, fans began to predict when we would clinch the pennant. That stretch of 10 games—after we'd been cold and the Orioles hot—was crucial. Denny McLain won three of them, lifting his record to 28–5. In two more starts, he would win his 30th.

Dobson won two consecutive games in relief in Oakland—the first on Bill Freehan's home run in the 10th. The second was a four-run rally against the A's in the ninth. We were again playing the caliber of baseball we had for most of the season, clawing until the final out. My biggest contribution during those 10 games was a three-hit 2–0 triumph over the California Angels, a game in which I struck out 12 and retired 20 in a row at one point. I lost my next start but then threw two consecutive shutouts as pennant fever embraced us all. "It happens every year," I told reporters after the 2–0 win. "The weather cools down, and here comes my sinking fastball. It acts like a 'dry spitter.'"

It was after this game that I began hearing questions about possibly getting a start in the World Series. "Yeah, I figure I might start Game 3 here," I said.

We hadn't clinched yet. But we were back on the right path—and would stay on it.

I also threw a two-hit, 6–0 shutout against the Angels in Anaheim on September 9. You know, I never threw a no-hitter in my career—or even a one-hitter. But this was one of my three career two-hitters. Two of them were for the Tigers, but to disprove the belief that I went a full year without doing anything right for the New York Mets in 1976, I pitched the last of my two-hitters for them.

The third of the three shutouts I threw during the pennant stretch was my best game of the season. Denny had won his 30th game the day before, so all the celebrities had left town. But my family was still visiting because it had been "Mickey Lolich Day" at Detroit's Croatian Hall.

"There must have been 500 people on hand for it," I said about the honor. "I didn't get much sleep."

So I was pretty tired when I took the mound on that Sunday against Oakland. However, after five innings, I already had nine strikeouts (en route to 12), so I did okay. There were two types of motivation at work for me in this game. We reduced our magic number to two by combining our 13–0 win with Baltimore's 2–0 loss. And my parents had never seen me win a major league game. So with them in the stands, I wanted to be at my best. The reason I said it was my best pitched game—despite allowing one more hit (three) than in my previous start—was that I gave up fewer line-drive outs.

In any case the stage was now set for us to win the pennant. All but one hurdle—actually doing it—had been cleared. Everything was coming together at the right time. Our starters were throwing well, and the hitters were pounding the ball. In our 13–0 win against Oakland, we even used a pinch-hitter late in the game for Freehan, who had already hit two home runs. With 12 games left, we knew we were going to win the pennant; it was just a matter of when. The Yankees were coming to town on a 10-game winning streak. Plus they'd swept us four straight (all by one run) in New York.

They would not want to watch us celebrate. But they would have to.

With a 9–0 lead by the second inning of our first game against the Yankees, it became pretty clear that at some point during their stay in Detroit, we'd be throwing a party. We scored four runs on four hits, a walk, and a passed ball in the first inning. We followed that with five runs on three hits, two walks, a hit batter, and a wild pitch in the second. So much for the Yankees being spoilers.

While cobwebs continued to envelop our bullpen, Hiller went the distance in the 9–1 victory for our 10th consecutive complete game. He did a fine job for us with three consecutive wins in September, by the way. Or as Don McMahon, one of our relief pitchers, put it, "that boy Hiller has done a fantastic job."

The Orioles also won their game that day, however, so all we did was clinch a tie. But that was fine with us. Time was entirely on our side. Earl Wilson was supposed to start the next night but had to be scratched because of a shoulder problem. Joe Sparma started for us instead.

"When they asked me if I wanted to pitch," Sparma said, "I said, 'You're damn right I do.'"

A crowd of 46,512 would eventually settle into the seats. Attendance would fall to 9,063 the next night, so that alone tells you that we wasted no time taking care of business. Stan Bahnsen started for the Yankees. He could be tough, but Sparma singled in Freehan in the bottom of the fifth, and with the tension increasing, we still led 1–0 after eight innings.

I sat in the bullpen much of the game, peering out from that cramped little cave down the left-field line. I knew I wasn't going to pitch and I liked the camaraderie in the 'pen. My choice might have been cigarette-related as well. But I wasn't the only one who smoked down there.

After allowing a leadoff single to Charlie Smith in the ninth, Sparma had pitched to within an out of clinching when Jake Gibbs singled in pinch-runner Dick Howser from second base to tie the game. Bummer. I was pulling for Joe to go the distance, and manager Mayo Smith obviously was, too, because he let him face the great Mickey Mantle after Gibbs tied the game. The gamble paid off when Joe struck out Mantle to end the top of the ninth.

Our party had only been delayed, however, not canceled. With the bases empty in the bottom of the ninth—just when it looked like we were headed for extra innings—Al Kaline drew a two-out walk, and Freehan singled him to third. Then we received word before our game ended that the Orioles had lost. So we'd already won the pennant before the outcome at Tiger Stadium was decided. But we wanted our celebration to be launched with a win. So did the fans. And everybody got what they wanted.

After a walk to pinch-hitter Gates Brown loaded the bases, Don Wert singled on a 2–2 slider to drive in Kaline from third with the winning run. Watch the replay of Wert's hit and you'll see while Tiger Stadium is exploding with joy because the Tigers had just won their first American League pennant since 1945, Tony Cuccinello—ever the conscientious coach—made sure Freehan touched third base while Kaline scored before letting him join the celebration. "Let's listen to the bedlam" was Ernie Harwell's famous call on the radio after the pennant-winning hit. "It was my favorite moment ever as a ballplayer," Wert said, "but I needed help to get from first base back to the dugout. Fans mobbed me."

Jubilant Tigers owner John Fetzer was dunked in the whirlpool. He later turned to Mayo and told him, "You not only won the pennant; you might have saved the city."

And, of course, there was champagne everywhere.

When George Kell welcomed me up on the stage in the clubhouse for a postgame interview, he introduced me as "Mickey Lolich, the guy doing all the spraying."

Who, me? I didn't do *all* the spraying, but I did much of it. And you know what? I enjoyed every dripping drop.

Chapter 4

Game 1

"He changed his clothes in a phone booth."
—first baseman Norm Cash

The only suspense emerging from the World Series opener was whether we'd still be shell-shocked in the second game after witnessing Bob Gibson's masterpiece. He simply overpowered us in the humid heat of St. Louis. It was surgically magnificent. The Cardinals ace struck out 17, walked only one, and allowed five hits in the 4–0 victory. The game was more one-sided than the score made it seem. We weren't ever in it.

I don't know what the matter was, but we just didn't play well. If we felt jittery, which it looked like we did, it was out of character. We were a pretty loose team. I thought it was one of our strengths. I also thought we were a confident team. But that side of us had been tested right away by Gibson's dominance.

That's what it had been, though—sheer dominance. Gibson owned everyone, and I mean everyone. For instance, before the World Series opener, I'd seen Al Kaline strike out three times in the same game just once in the six years I'd been his teammate, and that "one time" had been the only time for him since 1958. Though I don't actually remember Kaline striking out three times the first time, according to his game logs, it took place against Minnesota Twins pitcher Jim Kaat in 1966, the year Kaat won 25 games.

To Al's credit, however, he was the only one of our hitters to get an extra-base hit, a two-out double to left in the sixth inning that moved Dick McAuliffe to third to represent our only scoring threat. But it didn't matter. Gibson struck out Norm Cash to end the inning, the threat, and pretty much any chance of us doing any kind of damage against him. Our only hit after that was a leadoff single in the ninth by Mickey Stanley, after which Gibson fanned Kaline, Cash, and Willie Horton to close out the game with an impressive statement. "He's one of the greatest pitchers I've ever faced," Kaline told the *Detroit Free Press*. "I feel good I was able to get a hit off him."

"Somebody should have warned us that he changed his clothes in a phone booth before the game," Cash said of Gibson's superman powers in George Cantor's book, *The Tigers of '68—Baseball's Last Real Champions*. In addition to being dominated by Gibson, we'd been sloppy with three errors. But mostly we were just overmatched at the plate. Our only at-bat with a runner in scoring position had come after Kaline's double.

So if anyone had been asked at that point which pitcher was most likely to win three World Series games in 1968, Gibson would have been a wise choice. The flaw with such a thought was that it looked questionable if Gibson would have to make three starts. That's how bad we looked. We needed to step up our game to convince anyone after the opener that we'd win one game—let alone four.

No wonder the Cardinals already felt like they were the better team. "I thought of the Tigers as a good ballclub," Gibson said in HBO's documentary *A City on Fire,* "but probably not as good as some of the National League teams we have to face day in and day out. I went into [the World Series] with the cocky idea that they had to be thinking about us more than we had to be thinking about them."

Denny McLain had been our starter in the opener. It was a given that he would be. Denny had been the toast of Major League Baseball with his 31 wins. I finished the season strongly, but, man, he'd been good all year. What's more: it was easy to see how his 31 wins could have been 35 instead. Rookie Jon Warden won McLain's first two starts because of late heroics—a walk-off home run in the bottom of the ninth by Gates Brown in the second game of the season and then another walk-off home run from Horton in the bottom of the 10th against the Cleveland Indians at Tiger Stadium. Jose Cardenal had put the Indians in front 3–2 in the top of the 10th inning with a run-scoring single off Fred Lasher, and with two outs against the Indians' Eddie Fisher, we needed "instant runs," as Ernie Harwell would have said.

And, sure enough, we got them. Kaline walked, and then Horton came through for the dramatic win. Warden had retired the last two batters in the top of the 10th, so he got the victory.

It was weird that by the time Denny won his first game of the season, Warden already had three wins—on his way to only four for the season. "Yeah, me and Denny combined for 35 wins that year," I've heard Jon say in the years since.

McLain also could have won two more games at the end of the regular season, but we lost both by the same score (2–1). He allowed only one earned run in the two games combined. In any case Denny was the automatic choice to start the opener and through the third inning he had kept the Cardinals from scoring. Probably the highlight of the first three innings—the point at which Denny most looked like Denny—was when he struck out Mike Shannon and Julian Javier after Tim McCarver tripled with one out in the second. At that point, it looked like Gibson had met his match.

But McLain's control deserted him. In the fourth inning, he allowed a leadoff walk to Roger Maris and also walked McCarver after Orlando Cepeda popped up to first. Run-scoring singles from Shannon and Javier followed, with the added complication of an error in left by Horton allowing Shannon to score. Suddenly, the Cardinals led by three runs. Our sloppy defense continued the next inning with Cash's error on Maris' grounder to first. With no help from his teammates, Denny was struggling, but it wasn't until Tommy Matchick pinch hit for him in the sixth that he was done for the day.

After the game Denny went back to the hotel lounge to play the organ before a live audience—just as he had done the night before the opener. "Mr. Gibson was super today," he said. "I don't even feel bad getting beat by him."

Lou Brock accounted for Game 1's final run with a solo home run in the seventh off Pat Dobson. "The Tigers looked like a bunch of high school sophomores playing their first game for the varsity," Joe Falls wrote in the *Detroit Free Press*.

Not tiring despite throwing 144 pitches, an amount no starter would dare throw these days, Gibson was in command the entire way. He felt he had surprised us with his selection of pitches. "They were swinging at breaking balls as if I didn't have one," Gibson said.

Feisty Jim Northrup didn't gush about him, though. "We're not afraid of him," Northrup scoffed. "I'm anxious for the next time."

McLain said he didn't have any control even while warming up, so he wasn't stunned that he struggled. "When I tried to throw low and away, it was up and in," he said. "When I tried to throw up and in, it was low and away. My control was real bad."

He said the flaw was a mechanical one he would fix for his next start in Game 4. But that was too far away for us to think of at the moment. With a sense of shell shock lingering, we needed to bounce back in Game 2. That was my assignment.

Chapter 5

Figs and Fastballs

"You also threw a mighty fast fig."

—local bus driver

When I signed with Detroit in 1958, I had to look at a map to see where the hell it was. In fact, I had only a vague idea where anything outside Oregon was. I didn't know much about the Tigers as a team either. It's not as if I had always dreamed of playing professional baseball. I never collected baseball cards. For that matter, I never so much as held a baseball until the day my dad, who was a park superintendent, volunteered me as a 12-year-old fill-in for a game between 14-year-olds so that it would not end in a forfeit. One of the teams was missing a player, but I didn't even own a glove. I had to borrow one. When I was told I'd be playing right field, I remember saying, "Where's that?"

But later on, when we were getting trounced, I boldly claimed I could throw as well as anyone I'd seen so far, though all I'd ever thrown were rocks at a nearby creek and figs at a distant city bus from the roof of my grandfather's garage. Those figs proved hugely important in the development of my arm strength, however. After all, the buses I heaved them at were more than 150 feet away from the garage—across two vacant lots and then some. When I started throwing them as an eight-year-old, I could only get the figs halfway there. But by the time I was 10, I could cover the entire distance. That was the beginning of me being able to throw hard enough to pitch.

Years later, after I had retired from the big leagues, my father introduced me to the driver of one of the buses. They'd somehow gotten to know each other. "I liked it when the figs would begin to ripen," the driver said, "because they'd splatter against the side, and all we had to do was wash them off. But when they weren't ripe, they left dents that I had to explain to my boss. You threw a mighty fast fig."

As a kid I still didn't know the game of baseball, though. Even when I pitched for the first time in that parks game, I wondered why a batter was allowed to go to first base after taking four balls—and I'm not making that up. But, man, I could sure throw hard. When I threw my first pitch, the eyes of the kid batting grew to the size of saucers. I went on to pitch three innings—despite not knowing what an inning was.

My Uncle Frank was so impressed with how I did against the 14-year-olds that he signed me up for a team of kids my own age, and that's how I began playing organized ball. By my junior year in high school, I wanted to play in the majors. And by then, no one wanted to face me because I threw so hard, and scouts were watching me every time I pitched. In those years there was no draft at the major league level, so if clubs were interested, you'd sign where you wanted to play. I'd become a New York Yankees fan because they were the team on TV the most often.

Not only that, it seemed like Whitey Ford started most of the televised Saturday games, and because he wore No. 16, I began to wear No. 16. I still didn't know very much about Major League Baseball, but Whitey was a left-hander who got guys out, so he became my favorite player. I never imagined I'd someday beat him and the Yankees in a major league game.

It wasn't a case of a dream coming true, though, because I never dreamed it. Our dreams weren't as grand as that. I was the grandson of a Croatian immigrant who'd come to the United States to work in the steel mills of Pittsburgh but spent only a year there because he wasn't happy. It was hot and dirty in the mills, but a fellow Croatian in the early 1900s told him that not only was the lumber industry hiring out in Oregon, but also that foreigners were being treated well. They weren't being sworn at just because they spoke a different language. Plus they could make a decent wage.

That's how the Loliches settled in Portland. My grandfather, Mijo, then wrote back to his girlfriend in the old country, saying that if she would marry him he would send her a ticket to get on the boat to America, which she did. She took the boat, then the train, and they got married when she arrived in Portland. Eventually, he made enough money in the lumber business to buy a little dairy farm raising cows and selling milk. With a horse and a wagon, he had a milk route that he drove every morning.

I grew up wanting to be a mailman. I even took the test to become one at one point.

I loved those days of growing up. I was an only child but had so much family around me—grandparents, uncles, aunts, cousins. I was a third-generation Croatian, but sometimes Croatia was only a few doors away. In fact, my grandmother Lucy didn't speak a word of English. We lived in a Croatian neighborhood with Croatian stores around us. She could speak her own language at those stores with other women.

If she had to go to the department store in Portland to buy a new dress, she'd take my mother or my aunt to help. She would point out to them the one she wanted, and they would take care of the rest.

Even without speaking English, she loved to watch those old westerns on the tiny black-and-white television my grandparents had in the 1950s. But she didn't always understand what she watched. I remember her ranting and raving in Croatian about a show she had just seen. Oh, was she upset. "I watched a man get shot and killed yesterday," she was saying in her own language to her brothers. "But today I saw the same man on another show—and he was alive! How can that be?"

It was the age of relative innocence on TV with all its westerns like *Have Gun—Will Travel, Wagon Train,* and *Gunsmoke.* Lucy Lolich would watch them all—and try her best to understand them all. But darn it: if a man was shot on Thursday, he shouldn't be alive again on Friday.

Bless her heart.

Right-Handed Southpaw

I'm a right-handed person who became a left-handed pitcher. That sounds odd, I know, but it's true. I do everything right-handed, but I pitched left-handed. Had I not had a mishap as a child, of course, it would not have been that way. It's funny how that turned out, but there was nothing funny about it at the time. A motorcycle fell over on me when I was a little boy.

If it hadn't, I would have been Mickey Lolich, RHP instead of LHP. But who knows if I ever would have been the pitcher I turned out to be—or, for that matter, a pitcher at all.

I grew to love motorcycles, have owned several in my life, but there was no way to love what one did to me when I was two years old. To this day, I don't know who it belonged to. It wasn't my dad's or any other relative's. It was just there on the street, normal as can be, minding its own business but on the brink of changing my life. I was riding my tricycle (probably too fast) down the sidewalk near my house in Portland one day when I went off the curb straight into a parked Indian brand motorcycle. I was just a little guy at the time, and to me this was a huge machine. Unfortunately, I ran into the kickstand, which folded up and brought the bike down on top of me, breaking my left collarbone in two places.

Life continued on as normal, though, in that I was right-handed, and my right arm wasn't hurt. So I was able to do everything important I'd been able to do before—like eating. But my left arm was strapped across my chest, and, as my mother always said, I was at the age that little boys like to pick things up from the ground, such as rocks, and throw them.

I initially threw them right-handed for two reasons. 1) I'd never done anything left-handed and 2) I couldn't use my left arm even if I wanted to. But when I started physical therapy—I guess it was called that in those days—one of the arm motions they used rotated my left arm up over my head. Like a throwing motion. By then, however, I had developed total atrophy in my left arm.

So as I started gaining strength in it, my mother and dad resorted to something that probably would land them in jail in this day and age. At the very least, I'm sure it wouldn't be allowed. Someone somewhere would call it cruelty, but I don't remember thinking it was.

My parents tied my right arm behind my back so that I would be forced to depend on my left. It made me use my left side for everything. I still had the instinct to pick up things— even my toy trucks—and throw them. But with my right arm restrained, I switched to throwing them left-handed.

That went on for awhile. Eventually, I returned to having full strength in my left arm, which meant my right no longer had to be tied behind my back. But that's when my parents saw how my right/left preferences had developed. I ate right-handed. I also went back to using my crayons right-handed, but whenever I picked up something to throw, I threw it left-handed. That was the start of me becoming a left-handed pitcher. I graduated from throwing rocks as a left-handed little boy to baseballs as a left-handed pitcher. I continue to this day to be a right-hander in almost everything else I do and I always hit right-handed, including the only home run I ever had (in the 1968 World Series).

But anything that requires a power stroke, I do left-handed. When I use tools, for instance, I saw right-handed, including for precision cutting, but when it comes to pounding with a hammer, I do it left-handed. To some extent I became ambidextrous; when I played tennis growing up, I could hit a forehand both ways. Some people called it cheating because I didn't have to use a backhand.

I wasn't cheating, though. That's just the way I was after my injury as a two-year-old. However, I didn't know anything about becoming a pitcher back then because I didn't know anything about baseball. Sports meant nothing to my dad, so in my early years they also meant nothing to me. I was just happy throwing rocks and figs. There were no other children on my street to play with, so I ended up inventing games. Plus, there was a lot of fun stuff around my house to throw.

In addition to his fig tree, my grandfather always had a garden where he could plant flowers. He'd use a shovel, so there were a lot of dirt clods around. I know it doesn't sound like fun, but "toss the clod" was among my first memories of throwing anything. I don't think the game ever caught on—for some reason. But the collision with an Indian motorcycle was the reason I threw them—and everything else—with my left arm.

Dirt, rocks, figs, and fastballs—I grew up tossing them all as, I suppose you could say, a right-handed southpaw.

A Yankee Offer

Even growing up in Oregon, I was a New York Yankees fan, and Whitey Ford was my role model. And as fate would have it, the Yankees not only became interested in signing me, but they also offered me more money than the Tigers did. My dream could have come true. All I had to do was say yes to them.

So how in the heck did I sign with the Tigers instead?

Well, first of all, my father needed to understand that I couldn't really lose regardless of what decision I made. It wasn't just a matter of the most money wins. The Yankees were offering me $40,000 to sign, which was certainly good money back in 1958. The Tigers were offering me $30,000. Either amount, of course, would have been several years of salary to my father, who made $7,000 as a park superintendent. "You're going to pay my son that much money to play baseball?" I remember him saying to a scout, as if he did not believe it.

Dad was capable of doing the math, though. So to him, the difference between the two offers needed to be a huge consideration. According to inflation calculators, $40,000 in 1958 equaled $340,000 in 2017. According to those same calculators, the $10,000 difference between what the two teams were offering was the equivalent of $85,000 in 2017. Significant, in other words.

But the decision wasn't just about money. It was about my future as a pitcher.

There were times when I thought signing day couldn't arrive fast enough. There were other times when it was arriving too fast. But suddenly it came down to signing day on June 30, 1958. Both the Yankees and Tigers were coming to the house, but the Yankees had the first appointment. All the other teams were out of it. My Uncle Frank grew up playing baseball and hockey in high school with Johnny Pesky, who'd been in the big leagues for 10 years, and most of them were with the Boston Red Sox. So as the big day got closer, he called Pesky, who was back east at the time.

He told Johnny that I was leaning toward signing with the Yankees. "Let's talk about this a little bit," Pesky replied. "I've heard the Yankees already have their eye on this New Jersey kid Al Downing, and if they sign him at some point, Mickey could be in competition with Al throughout their time together in the minors. So you're going to have two left-handers going back and forth as projected stars for awhile. Whichever one gets the edge in development will be the favored prospect."

As it turned out, Downing didn't sign right away. He spent a couple of years in college, signed in 1961, and pitched for the Yankees that very same year. There was more to what Johnny told my uncle, however. "I have just signed with the Tigers," he said, "to manage their minor league team in Knoxville. I had a meeting with the Detroit organization before I signed and I can tell you that they don't have any left-handed pitching in their minor league system worth a damn. So my professional opinion is that even though the Yankees are offering more, Mickey should go with Detroit."

That changed everything. After talking to Pesky, my uncle immediately came over to our house to speak with my parents.

My dad was still focusing on the dollar difference between the offers, but my uncle told him not to. Uncle Frank wanted me to concentrate on the fastest path to the big leagues. I just wanted a career as a professional baseball player. But my mother didn't have the tunnel vision my dad did, so she turned to my uncle and said, "Okay, Frank, we'll go with Detroit."

The next day the Yankees scout came into our house with a smug smile on his face because he knew he had outbid the Tigers. My mother and dad were sitting there, but it was my mother who spoke. "Before you get carried away," she told the Yankees scout, "I have to tell you that we're going with Detroit."

The guy's jaw dropped to the floor. I think he was still mumbling in disbelief when he left. Then along came Bernie DeViveiros of the Tigers, being all courteous and cordial because he had an appointment but knew he was being outbid. When he came into the house, Bernie said, "As you know, $30,000 is all we can offer, so I suppose you signed with the Yankees."

That's when my mother said, "No, Bernie, we're going with Detroit." And his jaw set a modern record for how far it dropped.

"Really?" Bernie said.

"Really," my mother replied.

The $30,000 bonus from the Tigers was far from being a lump sum, though. Later, I found out that when Bill Freehan signed for $100,000, he got $100,000. But he got paid a salary in addition to his bonus. I received $10,000 a year, but the yearly amount was broken up this way: I received a bonus of $7,500 on January 1 for three years plus a salary of $2,500 for each of the first three seasons that I played in the minors.

That was Jim Campbell for you. He was always tough on the dotted line. But the reason I ended up with the Tigers in the first place wasn't a financial one. It was about the chance of getting to the big leagues faster. So I followed Pesky's advice and reached the majors, but it still took awhile to get there.

A Bloody Turn of Events

One of the most career-changing hits I ever allowed was a triple off my face. Despite being painful at the time, it proved to be an odd turning point that propelled me to the majors. In 1962 I was pitching for Denver in the Tigers' farm system. In a game at Louisville, I was facing Bob Boyd, who had been in the majors for several years with the Baltimore Orioles. He was still a fine hitter, but he was ending his career in the minors. The guy could flat-out rake, though. His nickname was "the Rope" because of all the line drives he had hit in his career.

However, misfortune struck quickly when he lit into one of my pitches. I didn't see the ball until it skipped off the grass in front of me. But I do remember it coming right at my face.

I turned my head to protect myself, but the ball struck me on the left side, ricocheting off my face to the right-field corner for a triple.

In other words, it clobbered me pretty good.

Because my left eye was full of blood and I still was unable to see out of it, I probably shouldn't have been, but I was back on the mound four days later. Not able to see out of that eye, though, I was unable to follow the flight of the ball to the plate. Bottom line, I was pitching in fear.

My control was horrendous for the next three or four starts after the injury. So was my ERA. Denver's general manager called the Tigers saying I couldn't pitch for him anymore because of what had happened. It was decided I should be shipped somewhere I could recover. That's when the Tigers tried to send me to Double A Knoxville, where Frank Carswell was the manager.

No way.

I told them I wouldn't report. I refused to pitch for Carswell, who had called me out in front of the entire team when I last pitched for him. So I packed up instead and went home to Portland, telling the Tigers I was retiring. I was only 21, but I was serious. I was going to become a mailman.

A few days later, a high-level amateur team in the Portland City League called me to come out and watch them play, which hadn't been in my plans. I was done with baseball. I was going to stay away from the game. I went but didn't take a glove. All I was going to do was watch, but I should have known something was up when the manager of the amateur team told me my dad was in the grandstand wanting to speak with me.

Yeah, he just happened to show up. I walked outside and said, 'Hey, Dad, what's up?"

"In all the years you've pitched, I've never asked you to do something for me," he said. "But I want you to go out there and pitch tonight for this team."

I had told him I was through with baseball. But he didn't want me to be. This was his way of trying to save my career. "I just want you to go out there one more time for me," he said. "The blood is out of your eye. You are seeing clearly now. I want to see what you can do."

I realized, of course, that this had been a set-up all along between the manager and my dad. But for my father, for whom it was uncharacteristic to talk about baseball, I gave in.

One more game. But only one. "Okay," I said.

Then I borrowed a glove, pitched five innings and struck out 16 guys in a row. Not 15? Well, one guy got on base because of a passed ball. So I struck out 16 guys to get 15 outs. That's when I said to myself, *Dad was right. I can see that now. This went well. But I'm still not going to Knoxville.*

Aware of what had happened, Tigers executive Jim Campbell called me the next morning. At first he tried again to get me to agree to Knoxville, Tennessee. I refused. So he changed his approach. "How would you like to pitch for Portland [a Kansas City A's affiliate]?" He said. "They want to borrow you. We can arrange it."

This time I agreed. I stayed in Portland and was able to get back on the mound. With that decision, my road to the majors not only resumed, but also got a big boost when Portland's pitching coach Gerry Staley, a former Tiger, taught me how to throw strikes with a sinking fastball. It was one of the great turning points of my career. It had such a positive effect that by the *next season* I was pitching in the big leagues for the Tigers.

But if I hadn't been hit in the face, I wouldn't have struggled for Denver. And if I hadn't struggled for Denver, the Tigers wouldn't have tried to send me to Knoxville. Connecting the dots—if Boyd's line drive had missed me, I might never have been a major league pitcher.

How weird is that?

Finally Learning to Pitch

I didn't learn anything in the minors with the Tigers. Not how to throw strikes. Not how to hit corners. Certainly not how to pitch. What I learned outside the organization proved far more valuable. Coming up through the Tigers' system, this is what they told me: "Throw as hard as you can for as long as you can."

That was it. I don't know what they told other young pitchers, but that's what they told me, and it nearly condemned me to a career in the minors. Here's the problem I faced: I didn't have a clue about how to be a pitcher. Thankfully, Gerry Staley came to my rescue. Meeting him was one of the great breaks of my career, maybe the most important one. When the Tigers lent me to the Portland Beavers in 1962 after I told them I was retiring and going home to become a mailman instead of reporting to Double A Knoxville, it became my good fortune that Staley was the pitching coach there.

I'd been a batboy in Portland growing up, so I was on familiar ground. It also helped that the team there was bad, so they picked me up as a hometown kid, thinking maybe I would put some people in the seats whenever I pitched. As a franchise, Portland was not averse to being creative in its efforts to boost attendance. In 1961, for instance, the Beavers signed Satchel Paige, who was 55 at the time. Paige struck out 19 in 25 innings for Portland, but he also allowed 18 runs. I don't know if I did or didn't help them on the attendance front, but one thing was for sure, I needed advice on how to pitch. I'd never gotten any from the Tigers.

Staley enjoyed some excellent seasons as a starter in the 1950s for the St. Louis Cardinals, but his last hurrah had been as a relief pitcher for a Tigers team that won 101 games in 1961. There was no Tigers connection between the two of us, but he took me under his wing all the same. As Portland's pitching coach, he went to the manager and asked him for permission to work with me. "This kid has an arm that's unbelievable," I remember Staley saying about me. "He can throw and throw and throw and has good shit, but he can't get it over the plate. Things are going so damn bad for us, would you mind if I work with him individually in the bullpen and try to teach him how to throw strikes?"

Apparently, that sounded like a good idea to the Beavers' manager, Les Peden. "Why not?" Peden said. "Maybe we'll win a couple of ballgames."

Staley was up front with his intentions. "I'm going to teach you how to throw strikes," he said. "You have a great arm, but you don't know what in the hell you're doing. Didn't anyone ever work on control with you in Detroit?"

"No," was my answer. No one had worked with me about throwing strikes. I told him that Stubby Overmire, a pitching instructor who was a left-hander, once said to me, "Mick, I was a shit-baller, and you throw BBs out there. I can't teach you anything."

I know it wasn't fun to play behind me back in those days. Gates Brown said it was too damn hot to stand in the outfield for hour after hour with me pitching in the minors. I might strike out 10 and walk 10. Gates also said, however, that I was a far different pitcher by the time I got to the big leagues.

I had a fastball and a curve when I started working with Staley, but I didn't know where anything was going. In an era before velocity guns, the first thing he told me was that he thought I was throwing close to 100 miles per hour. "But I'm going to take you down to 95-96," he said.

When I asked why, he replied, "because I'm going to make a sinkerball pitcher out of you. I'm also going to teach you how to hold a ball differently than you ever have. So if you think you're wild now, you won't believe how wild you are going to be the next couple of games. But you have to promise me that you will give me two weeks of doing it my way, no matter what happens. It's going to be so horrible to begin with that you're going to want to kill me in less than a week."

What Staley primarily did was change my grip to the smooth part of the ball—where pitchers used to throw a spitter. Suddenly what I was throwing had a tailing action to it. Gerry was right, though. It was horrible to begin with. I'd throw the ball over the catcher's head. I'd throw it 57 feet. I'd throw it four feet outside—all because the ball was slipping out of my hand.

One day I was down in the bullpen, though, and sensed I was getting really close to the kind of spin Staley wanted. Then he made one more adjustment with my wrist, and the damn bottom started falling out of the ball, making it tail to the outside corner. I said out loud, "That's it, right there."

The sinker became my strike pitch. I could throw it all day long. By the time the season ended in Portland, I was the best pitcher on the team—and I give Staley all the credit in the world for it. He changed me from being a wild left-hander into a strike-throwing major leaguer.

The following spring with the Tigers, I pitched 18 scoreless innings. Staley had been right. The sinker turned me into a new pitcher. I didn't make the club out of spring training, though. It was tough for rookies to do that back then. Plus Jim Campbell had been promoted to general manager and he was going to darn well show me who was boss because I had quit on the team the year before. He wanted to prove he had the power. So I was the last player cut in spring training. When I went to the manager's office to receive the bad news about being cut, Tigers manager Bob Scheffing wouldn't even look at me.

But when I got called up in May, Scheffing jumped up from his desk with a big smile on his face and he said, "Am I ever glad you're here. Man, I wanted to keep you in spring training so bad and kept fighting for you, but Campbell would not let me do it."

That's because Campbell wanted my ass in Triple A. When Frank Lary got hurt and I got called up in 1963, though, there was a 30-day rule at the end of which I thought I'd be going back down to the minors. But I was wrong.

Way wrong. I ended up staying in the majors 16 years instead.

Chapter 6

Game 2

"Beware of the pudgy left-hander."
—St. Louis Cardinals outfielder Roger Maris

I was ready to make my first World Series start—unless manager Mayo Smith changed his mind at the last minute, which I can now say he didn't do. But with Mayo, you could never be too sure. He switched his original rotation plans for the World Series so that Earl Wilson would start Game 3 at Tiger Stadium, where there was a better chance that his ability to hit the long ball would make a difference. It was a difficult decision for Mayo but not quite heads or tails. "Mickey pitches better at home than on the road," he said, "but Earl's bat is a big factor in our ballpark."

Eventually, he settled on me for Game 2 and Earl for Game 3. No matter what, I wasn't going to be nervous about pitching in the World Series. I knew myself. I was not a pitcher who got nervous. Fortunately, the weather was much cooler in St.

Louis for Game 2 than it had been for the opener. I've always preferred pitching in cooler temperatures.

And also fortunately, since we're talking about being cooler, Busch Stadium was still a natural grass ballpark. In all likelihood artificial turf wouldn't have been a problem in October, but turf could hold the heat of a sunny day anytime. Lou Brock told me that when the Cardinals switched to artificial turf from grass at Busch, day games would often be unbearable. In the clubhouse tunnel, there was a refreshing water trough. If playing in a summer day game, the Cardinals players, who were not scheduled to hit, would go straight from the field to the trough and dunk their feet—shoes and all.

Brock said the temperature coming off the turf would sometimes be 140 degrees, and after plunging their feet into the trough, the St. Louis players would return to their positions with water squishing in their shoes. By the time they'd come back in, their shoes would be dry. I don't think the trough was needed for Game 2, however.

I also didn't like hard pitching mounds. One of the first things we needed to check in St. Louis was the condition of the mound. That meant a lot to me. There were some mounds that were rock hard. Any time I pitched in Anaheim, for instance, I'd actually take a screwdriver out to the mound to break up the dirt in front of the rubber. Busch Stadium passed the test in that regard.

The only other variable to consider, prior to the start of Game 2, was how I felt. As I later told Tony Kubek on television, I almost had to be scratched from the start because of a groin condition that was bothering me. Not to be graphically specific, but it was accurately written in Jerry Green's book, *Year of the Tiger*, that my problem was a boil on my "whatchamacallit."

It was a bothersome boil, but I pressed on regardless. Decent temperature, check. Decent mound, check. A tolerable situation with my "whatchamacallit," check.

Besides, we couldn't afford to go two games down. Give me the damn ball.

Cardinals pitcher Nelson Briles retired us in order in the top of the first on routine outs, and I would have enjoyed matching that in the bottom half of the inning. But after I struck out Brock to start the inning—anything but a sign of what was to come with him, by the way—Julian Javier singled to left, and Curt Flood walked.

Brock hadn't liked the called third strike, but I was happy to get it. Such calls sometimes go your way; the next time they don't. There was another call in that inning, for instance, that caused me to glare. I never really yapped at umpires, but I was known to glare once in awhile. That didn't always indicate I was upset with them, though. It could have meant I was upset with myself. I was hard to read that way. Plus, I was always talking to myself on the mound. I was as bad as Mark Fidrych, except I only murmured. The Bird talked out loud.

I didn't know the St. Louis hitters, nor had I studied them. I walked out of our pitchers' meeting before the series because I didn't want to hear what anyone had to say. Telling me to come back, the coaching staff asked me, "Don't you want to know how to pitch 'em?"

"Not with the way you're talking," I replied. "It's all negative."

The entire meeting was about what not to do, but I played hunches all the time, telling myself, *This is the pitch I want to throw.* So scouting reports on opposing players didn't mean anything to me.

I roomed with Fred Gladding for five years. He wasn't on the 1968 team but had been with us through 1967. He once said to me, "Mick, the reason you might be successful is that you don't know who the hell you're pitching against."

There was some truth to that.

Helping me out in the bottom of the first in Game 2 after Javier's hit and the walk to Flood was an excellent catch in foul territory by Al Kaline on Orlando Cepeda's fly ball to right.

Almost like crossing off items on a checklist—from getting a good jump, running a long way to the ball, easily tracking it from the sun into the shadows, bracing himself in textbook fashion as he hit the barrier, to holding the runner at second with his throw—Al did everything right on the play. But he almost always did.

About the only time Kaline ever made an error was when one of his throws to third would hit a runner. But even that only happened a couple of times a year. His arm accuracy would be dead on, but a runner nearing the bag occasionally would get in the way. There wasn't much an outfielder could do to prevent that. Al was no exception.

With the help of YouTube 50 years later, I finally watched replays of the games I pitched in the World Series. The memories flooded back. I can't say I remembered precisely how good his play in the first inning of Game 2 had been, though. That's nothing against Al or the catch itself. It's just that I was sometimes so focused on what I needed to do next that I was in my own little world out there. After an out I'd instantly start thinking about the next hitter and the strikes I needed to throw to him. In others words, I probably didn't spend much time thinking about the amazing catch Kaline had just made.

Pitching coach Johnny Sain taught me that of the first three pitches you'd throw to a hitter, the first two had to be strikes. So I always concentrated on quick strikes. That explains, though, why I sometimes don't remember how well the defense played behind me. I was always turning to the next hitter. And trying to stay positive, of course. I could even turn minuses into pluses. Like once in awhile, I'd throw a ball past everyone to the backstop and I'd just excuse it as a shit pitch. But I didn't mind them. Shit pitches often jolted me back into throwing strikes.

Anyway, I allowed a couple of runners in the first inning of Game 2 but got through it okay. I didn't give up any runs. We were still tied. Willie Horton put us in front in the second inning with a one-out home run, and I settled down to retire the side in order. Maybe I was already settling down, period.

Or maybe I retired the side in order because of the help I got. Tim McCarver tried bunting his way on in the second, but Bill Freehan threw him out at first. Norm Cash *might* have pulled his foot off too fast on the play, but it didn't get called. Norm usually got away with pulling his foot off but not always, which I don't like bringing up because it was how we lost Game 5 to the Oakland A's in the 1972 playoffs.

George Hendrick of the A's, who was clearly out at first base, was called safe instead because umpire John Rice ruled that Cash came off the bag while making a good play on a throw from Dick McAuliffe, to whom an error was charged. Hendrick eventually scored Oakland's second run of the 2–1 game that knocked us out of the playoffs that year. After that we didn't come close to making the World Series again.

No, this series against the Cardinals was our big chance to win it all, and I needed to shut them down in Game 2 to get us back on track. But it wasn't as if I had to pitch a Gibson-like game. I couldn't look at it that way. I had to pitch my own game. Besides, I knew the Cards were already wary of me. From what I heard, it was Roger Maris who told his teammates before the series began that if the Cardinals were going to win it, they'd have to get around "that pudgy left-hander." Brock later told me that most of the talk at their hitters' meeting was about Denny McLain. There hadn't been much said about me or Wilson when Maris stood up and said, "If you don't pay attention to the fat guy, he'll shove the ball right up our ass."

In the third inning, we doubled our 1–0 lead on my home run. To be sure, that stunned everyone. Knowing how improbable it was that I would hit one, not even my wife was watching me at the plate. "When Jan Hiller, John's wife, told me what just happened," Joyce Lolich said, "all I could say was: '*What?*'"

I used Al's thin-handled bat, hoping it would help, which it might have. But I wasn't a hitter. My job was to pitch, and I can honestly say that before I hit that home run I had told myself to swing at the next pitch, no matter where it was. I have a photo that shows it was way out of the strike zone. I just tomahawked it. When I speak at banquets, or when I used to, I would tell audiences that I never hit another home run because when I got to third base I realized it was too far to run.

If you've ever watched the replay of my trot, did you notice that Tony Cuccinello, our third-base coach, didn't even extend his hand to shake mine as I went past him? Neither did I reach for his. I think we were both too surprised. Oddly enough, I hit a home run to dead center on my first swing of spring training the following year, and someone, probably Jim Northrup, said when I returned to the dugout, "What the hell is going on, Mickey? You becoming the next Babe Ruth?"

We were much more relaxed from the get-go in Game 2 than we'd been in the opener. That was the first noticeable improvement. Curt Gowdy even said so on the national broadcast.

We had known we'd gone into the World Series as the underdog because the Cardinals had won the year before. But the good thing was that we didn't react to losing the first game by feeling more pressure. That was important.

I know I wasn't feeling any pressure. But then I never did. If anything, I was too laid back—like I had a habit when I was pitching of not looking at the scoreboard to see what inning I was in. In most games—including this one—I wouldn't know the third and fourth innings from the fifth and sixth. They all just blended together. Yeah, I guess you could call me laid back.

Someone asked me during the World Series why my uniform number was 29. Instead of saying, "Heck if I know," my answer indicated just how much I always strove to take everything in stride. I wanted No. 16 because New York Yankees pitcher Whitey Ford was my hero. But No. 16 wasn't available when I came up to the big leagues. Phil Regan was wearing it. The equipment guys made it sound as if No. 29 would be a good one to have. I thought I was honoring a left-hander in Tigers history who they told me had been "pretty good." But I never found out who it was. What I think happened is that they gave me the number because it was available and they knew I'd just say, "Fine with me."

Anyway, to go with the home run Horton hit in the second inning of Game 2, and the one I hit in the third, Cash added a solo shot to lead off the sixth. But a 3–0 lead wasn't what I'd call safe yet. I suppose pitchers differ on the definition of a "safe lead," but I always thought of four runs as being a good cushion. With a four-run lead, solo home runs weren't going to hurt you much, so you'd begin to think when you were up by four, *I've got this one.* Anything north of four runs felt a lot better, of course. But I was at three, not four.

After Cash connected, though, McAuliffe came through with a two-run single to center to make it a 5–0 game in the sixth. Now I was feeling more comfortable. But the Cardinals had the kind of lineup that could hurt you quickly. I had to guard against that happening when we led by five. At the very least, I knew they wouldn't just roll over. In fact, not only did they score a run off me in the sixth, but it also looked like they might get more. But Mike Shannon hit into an inning-ending double play that was neatly started by Mickey Stanley at short.

When Mayo told me he was going to use Stanley—a terrific center fielder—at short, my comment was: "No big deal. He can do it." I have no doubt that Mayo's mind was already made up by the time he talked to me, but I think he felt even better about it after we spoke. If he didn't, he should have. I was a big supporter of the decision. It was no gamble as far as I was concerned.

Leading by four, but with the bases loaded and no outs in the top of the seventh, it looked like we were about to break the game wide open, though it didn't quite happen. A run that scored on Northrup's double-play grounder to short, however, stretched our lead to 6–1. There might have been some at that point who felt I didn't need to finish the game. I was not among them. Neither was Mayo. For one thing, I was getting the job done, so I had his trust. For another, even if my pitch count was climbing, which it was, I never worried about it.

We didn't pay as much attention to pitch counts as pitchers do today. One year, for instance, I started Opening Day for us in Washington. It was a game in which I walked five, allowed some hits—and threw 182 pitches. Imagine if anyone tried that now. Fresh from spring training, first game of the season, and you throw 182 pitches? Baseball was indeed different in my day.

When Mayo didn't make a move to take me out after seven innings of Game 2, I figured I was in it to finish it. Plus, I wasn't done hitting. Although not as shocking as when I hit my home run in the third inning, I stunned everyone again by singling to center with one out in the eighth. "You sure it's not his birthday today?" Harry Caray said about me on TV.

I didn't say anything sarcastic to Cepeda at first base when I got there, though. I only used to do that with Baltimore Orioles first baseman Boog Powell. Ol' Boog couldn't get a hit off me to save his life, but one time when we had a big lead and I somehow reached first base safely, I turned to him and said, "So how's your day going?"

"Shut up, you asshole," was the reply I not only got from Boog, but also the one I expected and deserved.

The Cardinals had scored all the runs they were going to get by the sixth inning, but we hadn't. With two outs in the ninth and runners at second and third, the Cards elected to walk Freehan on purpose and pitch to Don Wert. Unless a pinch-hitter was looking for a bat, I would follow Wert. Struggling at the plate until that point, Coyote (Wert looked like Wile E. Coyote of cartoon fame) foiled the Cardinals' strategy by drawing a walk on a 3–1 pitch from Joe Hoerner to force in a run.

I had a habit of smoking a cigarette between innings, but with Wert up, I put it out and had grabbed a bat like any on-deck hitter would. I was not "itching for another time at bat," as the national broadcasters said, however. I was itching to get the game over. A lot of players smoked back then, by the way. For me it was two packs a day for a lot of years. I've long since given it up, but I was far from being the only pitcher who'd grab a quick smoke. I never chewed tobacco, though. I tried it once in the minors, got sicker than a dog, and that was that. Never again. When I had a bad case of bronchitis a few years ago, I went through a lot of medical tests, but the doctors told me when the tests were over that they were surprised I'd been a smoker because I "have great lungs."

With the bases still loaded and us leading 7–1 in the ninth, I headed up to the plate again.

On the telecast I was called "Slugging Mickey Lolich" for the only time in my life. I would never have another day at the plate like this one—and it wasn't over yet. "Mickey hasn't been as overpowering today as Gibson was in Game 1," said Gowdy as Hoerner missed the strike zone on his first pitch to me. "But who is? He's been a superb pitcher, though."

It's Outta Here!

Nobody was more surprised to hit a home run in the World Series than I was. I couldn't remember hitting a home run at any other level of professional baseball. As a teenager I hit a few in high school and a few more in Babe Ruth ball, which also would have been in high school, but back then I pitched, I hit leadoff, and I could run.

Those were the good ol' days when bones didn't creak. One time I hit the first pitch of a game out of the park to dead center. My coach had just left the dugout to take his spot near third base when I headed up to the plate. We walked together for a few steps, but it was long enough for him to say, "Pick on a good pitch, Mick, and get this started for us. You need to get on base."

Then I hit the home run and saw him in the dugout the next inning. "I thought I told you to get on base," he kidded me.

But after I turned pro, I hadn't come close to hitting a home run—until I hit a big one. It doesn't get much bigger than Game 2 of the World Series. I tell people that I wanted to wait until there were millions of fans watching me on TV. I mean, why do it in Cleveland with only 6,000 people sitting in the stands?

Of course, some of you don't remember when American League pitchers batted, but those were the rules for most of my career. The designated hitter didn't come in until 1973.

What felt weird about the home run I hit off Nelson Briles in Game 2 is that I pulled the ball, something I rarely did. And I hit it hard, which I also rarely did. I was a right-handed batter and I'd usually hit the ball—when I hit it at all—to right field, right-center, or up the middle. Whenever I pulled it, the result was an easy out. But this time I pulled the ball with some pop.

"I knew I hit it good," I told reporters after the game. "I saw the left fielder go back, look up, and then I heard the crowd."

With the game being played in St. Louis, I think the reaction was mostly a gasp from the Cardinals' fans. They had to be shocked. I know I was. Just then, however, as I was losing sight of the ball, I stepped over first base. I hadn't actually seen the ball go out, so I didn't know that it had. If you watch the film, you can clearly see that I never touched the bag. But that was a habit of mine.

I'll be honest: whenever I was pitching, I never worried about hitting. Any time I'd hit a ground ball or a fly ball, I didn't make a point of stepping on the bag because you could turn an ankle and get hurt that way. With me not knowing for sure where the ball ended up when I hit it, I stepped over the base again. But as I went past him, I heard Wally Moses, our coach at first base, say, "It's outta here!"

"It's what?" I turned around and asked Wally. "What did you say?" I'm sure I also said something probably unprintable.

"It's outta here," Moses repeated.

Sure enough, it was.

On television, legendary broadcaster Harry Caray was just as surprised as everyone else. Nor was he hesitant to say so. "There's a long fly ball, way back, it might be out of here," Harry blurted out. "Home run! Holy cow! How about that one? Mickey Lolich, with one of the lowest lifetime batting averages in major league history, has just hit one out of the ballpark! You know, when he got to first base, it looked like he didn't believe it and was going to come back to the plate. Ah, that's what makes baseball the fascinating, unpredictable game it is."

Harry was right about me being a bad hitter. My major league batting average was an anemic .113 at the time. I had doubled three times in 1968 and tripled once in 1967, but, unlike my colleague Earl Wilson, a legitimate home run threat as a pitcher if ever there was one, it was understandable for opposing pitchers to consider me an easy out. Most of the time I was.

No wonder I couldn't believe what Wally was telling me at first base. *It's out?* The whole damn thing was pretty unbelievable. I made sure I went back to touch the bag, then started my trot around the bases. But it was slightly faster than a trot. I still couldn't believe I had just hit a home run in the World Series.

The pitch had been a high fastball, but one "without much on it," Briles said.

"Why, that pitch wasn't even a strike," Cardinals manager Red Schoendienst said. "It was head high."

Indeed it was. As I said at the time, I swatted at it "to get it off me" like I would a bee buzzing around my nose. Not only was it the first home run I had hit in the big leagues, it also was the first one Briles had allowed to a pitcher. So was he embarrassed by it? Nobody would have blamed him if he had been. "I never get embarrassed," he told reporters. "You have to give people credit sometimes. The batter had to hit the ball."

It was a comment to which I could relate. I gave up a lot of home runs in my career, many of them because I made a bad pitch. But the batter at the plate still had to hit the ball. This time, though, the batter was me.

When I checked my swing on a pitch out of the strike zone, Cardinals pitching coach Billy Muffett went to the mound. It's believed he said to Hoerner something like "Throw strikes, damn it." It's unknown what Muffett really said to Hoerner, nor is it important to know, but this was getting out of hand for the Cardinals. Wert had just walked with the bases loaded, and the count on me, "Slugging Mickey Lolich," was 2–0. On a full-count pitch, I walked to force in the last run of the game. We won 8–1.

If someone had told me ahead of time that I would pitch a complete game, I might have believed it. I had pitched complete games before—many of them, in fact. But to chip in with two hits, one of them a home run, plus a bases-loaded walk? C'mon.

When Kubek started to interview me after the game, he said he didn't know what to ask me about first—my hitting or my pitching. I got a kick out of the comment, but we pretty much kept it to pitching. It was then that I told him I nearly hadn't started the game and that the initial plan was for me to pitch no more than five or six innings.

So much for plans. That's what Game 2 seemed to be telling us about the World Series that was now tied. Anything at all was capable of happening.

Chapter 7

Learning Curve

"He's not that type of person. He doesn't throw at hitters."
—Minnesota Twins hitter Cesar Tovar

I was proud of my career. But coming clean after all these years, there is something I regret that I did as a pitcher. I hurt a hitter badly with a pitch, but it wasn't in the big leagues. It was as a teenager in a Babe Ruth League game. And it haunts me to this day because I meant to hit him.

The team we were facing had a guy who was a very good player, but he had a mouth on him—a loud, annoying mouth. He constantly ragged at me, ragged at me, ragged at me. I don't remember his name, but he was on my ass all the time. I'm a pretty calm person and I was even then, but he took it too far. So when he came up to bat for what I thought would be the last time in the game, I decided I was going to stick a pitch in his thigh. Believe me, I wasn't someone who threw at hitters on purpose, but this time I was going to. Well, I threw the pitch, and it did not do what I wanted it to do. It hit him on the left side of his jaw. I remember thinking, *Oh my God, I didn't mean to do* that!

I ran to home plate, and when I got there, he was bleeding from his nose, from his ear, from his eye…and he was bleeding from his mouth. I felt like a total piece of shit. That's the only way I can put it. The worst thing about it is that the kid was one hell of a ballplayer and he never played baseball again. I broke his cheek and screwed up his eye. That's why he was bleeding from his eye. The pitch changed both our lives. I never threw at another hitter before I got to the majors. And as a major leaguer, I wouldn't throw at someone even when I was ordered to. I don't know how many times in my major league career, especially when I was around Billy Martin, that a manager told me, "I want you to drill so-and-so," only to have me reply, "No, I won't. I won't throw at anybody."

The response was always the same, not just from Martin, but from my other managers as well. They'd say, "What do you mean you won't? I'm the boss. I want you to throw at that son of a bitch." Martin went a step beyond that. He said, "It will cost you $100 if you don't drill him—and if you don't do it the second time I tell you to, it will cost you $200. It will keep going up."

I didn't care. I refused to throw at hitters.

With each angry manager, of course, I'd be called into his office after the game and he would say, "When I tell you to do something, you better do it. I'm running this club, not you."

They'd be very adamant about it. And basically they all said the same thing. They gave the orders. But they couldn't make me throw at anyone intentionally. That's what I kept saying to them. Then I would tell them the story about the kid in the Babe Ruth League that I hurt. After that every manager would say, "Now I understand."

To be completely honest, though, I did hit one more guy on purpose. It was my nemesis, Cesar Tovar of the Minnesota Twins, in 1969. But by then I had better control than I did as a kid. I knew the pitch would not get away from me the way it had years before.

Tovar owned me. He was the hardest guy for me to get out. He hit .419 in his career off me. From 1966 to 1971, it was worse than that. In those years he hit .478 (29-for-62) off of me. The ease with which he got on base against me, though, was not why I did it.

Pitchers are only human. They can take a beating. They can tolerate being taunted. It's part of the game. But they don't like to be shown up, regardless of the circumstances. And that time in 1969, it looked like Tovar was showing me up when he stole third and then stole home on the next pitch. That entire sequence was aggravating, however. Tovar had singled in his second at-bat after getting a double in his first. He was always getting hits off me, no matter where I threw the ball.

Trying to keep him close to the bag at first, I balked him to second, and then he stole third as I walked Rod Carew. But it didn't end there. Tovar stole home on a double steal, and then Carew, who had stolen second, also stole third and home. It was not my favorite inning of all time, I can assure you. But we won the game pretty easily (8–2). I wasn't embarrassed by the multiple thefts. If anything, I think I said at the time I was flattered because the Twins were basically telling me they couldn't hit me. So they had to create other ways to score. Actually, it bolstered my confidence against them.

All those stolen bases took place in the third inning, and when Tovar was in the on-deck circle again in the fourth, Martin, who was a rookie manager with Minnesota at the time, yelled to him from the Twins' dugout: "You better watch out, Lolich is going to get you."

Tovar's answer to him was: "No, he won't, he's not that type of person. He doesn't throw at hitters."

Billy replied, "But I think he will this time. He's going to get you."

And I got him, though I said at the time that the pitch simply got away and I hadn't meant to hit him. But I had. I hit him on the hip. I heard he carried the outline of the baseball's seams on his hip for four days. The two teams were warned by the umpires after Twins pitcher Dave Boswell later brushed back Al Kaline. But that's as far as the bad blood went. It never bubbled over into a brawl.

Tovar was correct in what he had said to Martin, though. I didn't have a reputation for throwing at people. I never caused any trouble. Over the years I hit guys because as a rule I pitched inside. To be a successful pitcher, you had to. One year (1965) I even led the American League in hitting guys. I hit 12 of them. My teammate Dave Wickersham was second with 11, and another teammate, Hank Aguirre, was third with 10. We all pitched inside that year. But we weren't headhunters.

In 1969 I hit 14 hitters—the most I ever hit in a season— but I didn't lead the league. Far from it. Tom Murphy of the California Angels hit 21. For some reason, though, I was real wild that season. I also set a career high with 14 wild pitches and 122 walks. But my other numbers were good (19–11, 3.14 ERA), so it ended up being a strange, yet a good, year.

It was strange because I hit someone I meant to hit for the first and only time as a major leaguer. It was good because I hit him where I meant to hit him—unlike that terrible day back in Babe Ruth ball.

Bad Blood

I never had anyone charge me at the mound. Probably the closest I ever came to causing a brawl occurred on a day when roles were reversed, and I was the one who got hit by a pitch.

We were in Cleveland to face the Indians on a Sunday in 1971. I hadn't been at the first two games of the series, though, because my wife, Joyce, was in the hospital back in Detroit. I didn't travel until it was my day to start. In the first inning, I nicked Chris Chambliss, the Indians' first baseman, on the hand with a fastball up and in. Nothing came of it, though. Chambliss just went to first. But then I got drilled in the hip on purpose (by Indians starter Steve Dunning) when I came up to bat. "Yes, I hit him on purpose," Dunning admitted later about the incident. "You have to protect your players."

Ken Suarez was the Indians catcher at the time, so I turned to him and said, "What in the hell was all that about?" He quickly referred to the brawl that happened earlier in the series, saying, "With all that stuff about guys getting knocked down and pushing each other, we're not going to put up with any crap if you're going to start it again. So you got nailed for hitting Chambliss."

I told Suarez, "I wasn't even here for that. But if you guys want to play that way, I'll play that way."

The altercation between the two teams that weekend had been a nasty one caused by pre-existing bad blood and by Cleveland's catcher Ray Fosse getting hit with a pitch by relief pitcher Bill Denehy in the opening game of the series. When Fosse charged the mound, Denehy bloodied him with a gash to the neck. Other brawlers included outfielder Willie Horton, who "went after half a dozen Indians himself," according to Jim Hawkins' account in the *Detroit Free Press*, and infielder Ike Brown, who was "bobbing and weaving and doing his best to make the crowd forget Muhammad Ali."

Said Tigers manager Billy Martin of Horton and Brown, "It was just a matter of stopping them from kicking the hell out of Cleveland's whole team."

Denehy, meanwhile, didn't mince words about the way he chose to defend himself at the mound. "When Fosse came at me, he was fair game," he told Hawkins. "I just tried to kick him in the face. If he had gotten hold of me, he might have killed me."

But a kick to the face? It was a brutal brawl, for sure—one that prompted Jim Honochick to call it "the bloodiest I've seen in 23 years as an umpire." But it also caused Indians manager Alvin Dark to say that Horton needed to be suspended for being "overactive" and for some Cleveland players to predict that the lingering bad blood had a chance of boiling over again.

When I got hit by Dunning in retaliation for hitting Chambliss, tempers were tested.

Or so it seemed. But I think it defused the situation when, instead of getting angry, I shrugged my shoulders. I hadn't come to Cleveland, remember, until it was my turn to pitch. Hearing that, Suarez tried to reduce the tension on the Cleveland bench. He turned to his dugout, waved his arms, and yelled, "He knows nothing about this stuff!" But he also told me, "We don't want to get into it with you because you throw so damn hard."

After that, there were no more problems. I was hit by a pitch five times in my career—four times as a Tiger and once as a New York Met. I didn't do much as a hitter over the years, but eventually filled in many of the blanks next to my name.

I tripled twice, hit one sacrifice fly, stole one base, was caught stealing once—and hit the only home run of my career during the 1968 World Series against St. Louis. Also, I was caught stealing once. The record shows I was caught trying to steal third in the fifth inning of a game in 1968 that we lost 3–2 in Chicago against the White Sox. I don't remember it, but a pitcher getting thrown out while trying to take third in a game we lost by a run doesn't sound like the smartest play in the world. Fortunately, we were 40–22 at the time. And the blunder was never mentioned again—until now.

Home Cooking

If you ever saw me pitch in the big leagues, you know that for much of my career, I didn't need to gain weight. I'd already gained it. I had a belly on me. No secret there. At times it was even referred to as my "famous" belly and, well, it just sort of became my look. I was the beer drinkers' hero.

But at one point in my career, the Tigers were worried about me being too thin, not too heavy. I'd been skinny in high school and as a minor leaguer I was still pretty skinny. When I was 21 in 1962, I left the Tigers' minor league team in Denver because of a disagreement over a demotion I was about to get. However, while arranging that my hometown Portland team could borrow me, Tigers general manager Jim Campbell gave me some advice to follow while I was out there. "Eat," he said. "Put on some pounds."

I went into pro ball weighing 165 pounds. After three years I was up to maybe 170 but no higher than that. Now I was going home for awhile, and Campbell wanted me to gorge on my mother's home cooking. He didn't have to tell me twice. When I reported to spring training the next year, I weighed 185 pounds. To Campbell—and to me—that was just fine.

Eventually, my weight surged well past 200 pounds, giving me my "ample gut" as it often has been described. But I always maintained a good attitude—and my sense of humor—when asked about my weight. "Big bellies run in the Lolich family," I said after the 1971 season in which I won 25 games. "We're healthier when we are chubby."

First Win

In case you were wondering—but even if you weren't—my first major league win occurred in the second start of my career on May 28, 1963, against the Los Angeles Angels.

I had to look up the date, but I didn't have to look up the location. The game was played in Los Angeles, not Anaheim, because the Angels didn't move into their own ballpark until 1966.

We stayed at the Ambassador Hotel in L.A., and the early story in the Detroit papers the next day was that I nearly didn't make it to the game. Joe Falls of the *Detroit Free Press* wrote that as I was leaving to get on the team bus I didn't notice a helicopter that was landing on the helipad there. Which means, of course, that I didn't duck. Joe wrote that it was a close call, and, while I don't remember how close, I can safely say this: leaving the hotel to make only my second major league start, I doubt I would have been on the lookout for helicopters. In fact, a flying saucer could have landed next to me, and I probably would not have noticed.

I'm sure the task at hand pretty much dominated my thoughts. I was 22 years old, had never been a particularly good minor league pitcher, and was about to face a bunch of major leaguers, most of whom I knew nothing about. We had lost my first start (4–2 against the Orioles in Baltimore on May 21) and were struggling as a team, 11½ games out of first place already. So I really wanted to help turn it around.

The only hitter in the Angels' lineup I even remotely knew was George Thomas because we'd both been in the minors with the Tigers. But Albie Pearson leading off? I knew nothing about him. I didn't even know that he was only 5'5". Leon Wagner batting third? Knew nothing about him either. In fact, when I made that start against the Angels, I did not know anything about anyone I was pitching against—except George.

Then again, back in those days we didn't have extensive scouting reports. It was mostly word of mouth about what individual hitters liked and didn't like. What's more, I was taught by an amateur pitching coach, a man by the name of Ed Demourest, that the best approach to any ballgame—no matter who was at the plate—was simply to throw the pitch that seemed to be the most appropriate at the moment. I was told that if a pitcher throws the pitch he wants to throw, regardless of the hitter, it's going to be 75 to 85 percent effective. But if someone makes you throw a pitch you don't want to throw, it'll be only 50 percent effective. That's what I was taught in Babe Ruth ball back home in Portland, and it's the philosophy I took into the big leagues. I was going to throw what I wanted to throw. So that—and the uh-oh factor of not knowing anyone I was pitching against—was most likely what was going through my mind. But, to be honest, it was all a blur.

When asked years later, I even had to look up who my catcher was to be reminded it was Gus Triandos, a guy who'd been around for several years. Gus caught me a lot that first year. But if he wanted me to throw a curveball and I wanted to throw a fastball, I'd shake him off. Even then, in just my second start, I'd shake him off, and he hated it when I did. Gus was the veteran; I was the rookie. But if I had a pitch in my head that I wanted to throw, that's what I threw. It's the way I pitched my whole career.

Was I nervous? No. Looking back at my game logs, you can see that I already had pitched in relief a couple of times for the Tigers and that I had started in Baltimore. So this wasn't my major league debut. But I wouldn't have been nervous even if it had been. I hadn't been nervous in Baltimore either. That's simply not the way I was. I never got nervous.

But there were some bumps to get over. Pearson led off with a single against me. Then I hit George Thomas, who was followed by Lee Thomas in the Angels' lineup. I wild pitched the runners to second and third but got out of the first inning with a grounder to second. I later threw two wild pitches and also hit two batters, but I somehow got through it all to throw a complete game. And the Tigers won 3–1. Dick McAuliffe hit a two-run home run to help us out. We played pretty well for a couple of weeks after that, but a 10-game losing streak in June set us back. A defeat in my first start at Yankee Stadium against my idol Whitey Ford was one of those losses.

I was still looking for my first win in that Angels game, though. I don't remember the sequence specifically, but according to the box score, I retired the side in order in the second inning, and all the outs were on ground balls. Buck Rodgers hit one to third, Bob Perry hit one to short, and finally Jim Fregosi hit one to short.

That means my fastball must have been sinking. Even then, I was basically a sinkerball pitcher—and remained that way for much of my career. I was the same pitcher throwing the same pitches in 1968 that I was in 1963. I didn't change until I added the cutter in 1971. But as excited as I was to be in the big leagues, I knew I was only up because of Frank Lary's ongoing struggles. I also knew there was no guarantee how long I'd last. So I just wanted to make a good impression. A quick, good impression would be even better.

We had some real good veteran pitchers on that team, but they didn't mix with us kids—like I don't remember any interaction at all with Jim Bunning. He was the club's aristocrat, and I was a punk kid, staying in my own little corner. Hank Aguirre also was on that team and, while I grew to love Hank, even he didn't say much to me right away. Those guys were established. They weren't concerned about the likes of me.

A few things went wrong, but a lot went right in my first win. I'm proud I hung in there to pitch a complete game. I always liked finishing what I started. I was like that my entire career.

But the Angels went 0-for-9 with runners in scoring position. So when the going got tough, I guess I must have, too.

That first season in the big leagues was a roller-coaster for me. I threw three more complete games, ended up with a 5–9 record, and discovered that—like anyone else—I needed runs to win. I went 0–6 when the Tigers scored fewer than three runs. The game that hurt the most that first year was a one-hit shutout I took into the ninth inning in late July at Baltimore. I lost it 2–1 on a two-run, two-out pinch-hit home run by former Tiger Dick Brown. My mistake was to come in belt high to Brown after being specifically told by manager Charlie Dressen to keep the ball down. That should have taught me to follow orders.

But in many ways, that game was important for me—and for those just getting to know me. For instance, even though I was a rookie, people could see I was a calm competitor. Falls wrote: "Mickey Lolich, who is about as carefree as Mickey Mouse, pitched the most spectacular game of the Tigers' season Monday night—and lost. But it was a hugely important game for him. It was the game in which the young left-hander grew up. The Orioles poured out of their dugout and mobbed [Brown] when he reached the plate. They all but carried him off the field. Lolich? He simply walked from the mound. No histrionics. No dramatics. No glove-slamming theatrics. In this moment of despair, the boy became a man."

I don't know about that, but I was an unemotional player pretty much my whole career. I never yelled at umpires. Never got upset. Didn't show much emotion. Not everyone liked me being that way. But somebody must have. I stuck around a long time.

Bringing the Heat

I haven't ever been the kind of guy to do something just because it was the accepted way to do it. I really wasn't interested in the accepted way. I had my own way. And my own way worked for me. For instance, I never iced my arm. I boiled it in the shower. Some might say I scalded it. And they weren't far wrong. "I don't know how he could stand it," said teammate Jim Price.

Seriously, I never believed that a pitcher needed to apply ice to his arm after a game. That was always the thing to do, though. It was the accepted way. Wrap it in ice. But I believed heat was the answer. Ice did nothing for me. People always asked me—they ask me still—why I never had a sore arm. I threw a ton of innings and made hundreds of starts in my career, yet I missed only one start that I can recall because of an injury.

It wasn't soreness caused by overwork, however. In 1969 I got hit on the left forearm in Oakland by a line drive, forcing me to leave the game in the fifth inning. It had nothing to do with fatigue or dead arm. I came home from the West Coast, skipping a start in Seattle, but when I returned to the mound 13 days later, I tied my own team record with 16 strikeouts.

I just never had any arm trouble and I believe it's partly because of my postgame routine. Instead of icing my arm, I'd run it under the hottest water I could stand for at least 15 minutes. I'd get into the shower and turn the water temperature up as high as I could tolerate. Then I'd stand there until I knew it was cooked. By the time I was done, my arm would be scary looking. Ask anyone. "It looked like a lobster," said former Tigers manager Jim Leyland, who sometimes caught me in spring training. "After boiling it in the shower, his arm looked like a cooked lobster. Two days later, though, he'd be throwing on the side, normal as all get out."

I never tried to convince anyone that my way was the right way for them. A lot of people thought I was crazy to stand under a stream of hot water and, I mean, *really* hot water. I'm just saying it was right for me.

Chapter 8

Game 3

"Earl, did you hurt yourself?"
—catcher Bill Freehan

I needed to do some fence mending before this game. A newspaper story had been written, claiming that I called Lou Brock a showboat for stealing second base in Game 2 when the St. Louis Cardinals were five runs down. I hadn't said any such thing, so I called over to the St. Louis clubhouse when I got to Tiger Stadium. Lou came to the phone, and I told him not to believe the story. He said he didn't. "I've been in the majors six years," I told him, "and I've never said anything about another player."

It didn't last long, but we had a good conversation. When we were about to hang up, Lou said he put the blame on "dumb newspapers." But it was good to get that bit of business out of the way and focus entirely on the upcoming games. After we won the second game, at least we knew we'd be playing our full complement of home games—in other words, all three. And as far as the starting rotation was concerned, I knew I'd be getting a second start in Game 5.

Of course, heading into Game 5, we didn't know if we'd be up 3–1 in games, down 3–1, or tied, but no one was looking that far ahead anyway. We just felt good about playing the next three games at home. Now all we had to do was get through the off day without going crazy.

Anyone who's played in the World Series will tell you that one of the toughest parts of it is making sure that all your relatives and close friends are taken care of with tickets and a place to stay.

Jim Leyland once said, "It's a party for them, but it's strictly business for those in uniform. The first off day can wear you out if you aren't careful."

I second that motion. What we did was to put our entire family up in a hotel instead of opening up our house to a big crowd. Joyce and I stayed there, too. It was a wise move.

Seeing Tiger Stadium all dressed up for Game 3 was wonderful. It wasn't even called Tiger Stadium the last time Detroit had been in a World Series. It had been Briggs Stadium. The city sure was excited. And the ballpark looked great with bunting displayed all around.

Big Earl Wilson got into some trouble in the first inning. It was familiar trouble, though. Brock walked to begin the game and stole second. He had run us ragged in the first two games and clearly wasn't about to stop. He would steal three bases in Game 3. "I've never seen anyone disrupt a game the way he does," Al Kaline said. Dick McAuliffe was more blunt with his comments, firing a shot across the bow of our pitching staff. "I just wish these guys would concentrate more on the hitters than on Brock," he said.

Curt Flood followed with a walk, but on a strikeout of Roger Maris, Brock was thrown out trying to steal third. Orlando Cepeda ended the inning with a grounder to short. Wilson was jittery, allowing seven base runners—four of them on walks—in the first four innings. But he was getting the job done, and by the end of the fourth, we had a 2–0 lead thanks to Kaline's two-run home run off Cardinals starter Ray Washburn in the bottom of the third.

On a pitch to Flood in the top of the fifth, though, Wilson's right leg buckled. When Bill Freehan asked if he had hurt himself, Wilson replied, "Yeah." Earl stayed in the game, and it's easy to look back and say this now, but the fact is...he shouldn't have. "To me, it was a game like any other with one difference," Wilson said. "I couldn't get the ball over the plate. The ball felt slippery to me for some reason. I had trouble gripping it. But that's not an alibi."

When Maris walked after Flood's RBI double, Mayo Smith went to his bullpen. It was a move he had to make—given that Wilson was hurting—but waiting until someone had to come in to face a ready-made jam was not one of Mayo's best decisions. (He didn't know it at the time, but Wilson was done for the series.) With two outs and a run in, Tim McCarver belted a three-run home run off Pat Dobson to give the Cardinals a 4–2 lead. It wasn't as if McCarver crushed the ball to right, but it had the same effect as if he had. "It would have been a routine out in St. Louis," McCarver said. "I didn't hit it too well. It wasn't even a strike."

McAuliffe countered with a solo home run in our half of the fifth off Washburn, who had trouble throwing his curve on the chilly day. But of the pitching conditions in general, he said, "It was pretty nice out there."

It was a one-run, up-for-grabs game at 4–3 after McAuliffe connected. And we would soon get a chance to tie it. With one out in the sixth, Washburn walked Norm Cash and Willie Horton, putting the tying run on second base for us. At that point the Cardinals went to Joe Hoerner, who'd had a rough time with his control, including a bases-loaded walk to me in Game 2. This time, though, he got the job done. Jim Northrup popped out, and Freehan flied out to left. It was our last good chance to take the lead. Hoerner went on to toss three and two-thirds innings of scoreless relief, calling the appearance "the happiest moment of my life" because his parents were in the crowd.

Meanwhile, the Cardinals stretched their lead to 7–3—which would be the final score—by jumping all over Don McMahon in the seventh. McMahon had gotten through the sixth easily enough—he even struck out Brock—but in the seventh, Flood singled, Maris doubled, and Cepeda hit a three-run home run.

Known for struggling in previous World Series, Cepeda called it the biggest hit of his career. "I hit it for my mother, I hit it for my brother, I hit it for all the people in Puerto Rico," he said. "I hit it for my teammates, I hit it for myself. I am happy, I am glad."

But we weren't happy and glad. Not only had we lost the game, we were about to face Bob Gibson again. "You know, he's not Superman," Mayo said. "He's gotta get beat sometime."

That's true. But we weren't entirely sure Game 4 would be the time.

Chapter 9

Fun and Games

"I'm outta here, right?"

—Mickey Lolich

Of all the managers I played for, Charlie Dressen kept track of his players the closest, constantly wanting to know where they had been and what they were doing. As he once said, "You have to get your rest in order to play hard."

Charlie was a smart baseball man. I learned that right away. But he also was a snoop—not to mention an unforgettable character, a man whose philosophy was: "I want the team to run like hell, slide like hell, and play like hell."

The problem, though, was that we'd been losing like hell. We were in ninth place, next to last. So when the Tigers in 1963 were on the brink of firing popular Bob Scheffing—an easygoing man who once said, "Of course, I feel bad about losing, but I don't die about it"—they brought in Charlie to help analyze why the team was off to such a bad start.

Soon after that, he became our manager.

He'd been around the game a long time, knew his baseball, and was very observant. To his credit, he noticed a flaw in my delivery right away. He said I was tipping my pitches. Nobody else had ever told me that. With my old-time windup, I was bringing my hands high up over my head whenever I was going to throw a fastball. But when I was going to throw a curve, I kept my hands lower. I pitched with his advice in mind the rest of my career. Charlie also gave me a world of confidence by saying early on that I was going to be one of his starting pitchers in 1964. He didn't have to make that commitment. With a 5–9 record as a rookie in 1963, I hadn't really proved anything.

An opening in the rotation was created, though, when the Tigers traded Jim Bunning during the offseason. Charlie didn't like how often Bunning used his slider. He wanted him to depend more on his curve, and when Jim stubbornly refused, the Tigers traded him to the Philadelphia Phillies. The front office initially wanted Felipe Alou and hoped to get him from San Francisco at the winter meetings, but the Giants traded Alou to the Milwaukee Braves instead. Two days later, Bunning was dealt to Philadelphia, where he had a lot of success and eventually became a Hall of Famer. In return we received outfielder Don Demeter, who didn't live up to expectations in Detroit.

There were other pitchers who got a chance to start in Bunning's absence in 1964, but fortunately I made the most of the opportunity by winning 18 games. I'm glad Charlie wasn't a vindictive guy because one day in my rookie season I gave him ample reason to dislike me. I was struggling in a game, but I didn't want to come out. So when he began walking to the mound with intentions of removing me, I started imitating something I saw Phil Regan do in my first year with the Tigers.

Trying to show Dressen I was agitated, I began to bounce the ball on the pitching rubber as he got near. But instead of bouncing straight back to me, the ball hit the edge of the rubber and caromed off at an angle, hitting Charlie you know where— right where it would hurt the most. Yep, the jewels. Down to his knees he went in pain. I wasn't sure what to do. But what I did probably wasn't the best thing: I headed toward our dugout. "I'm outta here, right?" I called back to my manager as he groaned on the ground. Meanwhile, all the players in the dugout were laughing like hell. Fortunately he knew I hadn't done it on purpose.

Seeking Protection

Just about every part of my body, sooner or later in my career, got hit by a batted ball—so much so that eventually my first reaction to any liner hit back at me was to get out of the way.

So instead of trying to catch line drives, unless I was protecting myself, I just figured I'd make up for it by striking the next guy out. But even while getting out of the way, you can get hit. Left leg, right leg, shoulder, foot, hip, knee, you name it. Dick Allen even hit the *button* on the top of my cap one time in Chicago.

But the area I was worried about the most was, uh, between my legs. That's because I never wore a cup when I was on the mound. I couldn't wear one and pitch comfortably. A cup always dug into my left thigh on my delivery and would hurt like a son of a gun. So when I was pitching, I was out there unprotected. But that's why I developed a potbelly as an overhang. There were parts of me I wanted a roof over. That's what a good farmer does, right? He builds a shed for his equipment. My potbelly was my shed. Fortunately, despite everything that hit me over the years, I was never hit *there*.

I had some scary close calls, though. One in particular. Mickey Mantle hit a screamer at me one time, a liner I couldn't get out of the way of in time. Luckily, it hit the inside of my leg on its way to right-center for a base hit. I'm not sure I ever really saw the ball. I just heard it buzz. Then I started feeling some burning action and I thought to myself, *My God, it did hit me!*

Freehan came rushing out to see how I was. "You okay? How do you feel?" he asked.

"I think my stomach is up by my heart," I said.

The umpire was concerned, too, and said: "Man, he hit that hard. Take as much time as you need, Mick."

My leg bore the brunt, but better my leg than not my leg, if you know what I mean. I took the umpire up on his offer of extra time between pitches. He helped out by dusting off the plate a time or two, but eventually I gave him the nod that I was ready. Yep, of all the close calls I ever had, that was the closest.

Charlie liked to keep his players in line, though. On the road, he'd give the hotel elevator operator two baseballs—one to keep but another one to return to him the next morning.

The only rule was that the operator couldn't ask for autographs until the team curfew expired at midnight. So when Charlie went down first thing in the morning to retrieve his signed baseball, he read the signatures and instantly knew who had come in late. That's how he found out who to fine for breaking curfew.

Charlie used other tricks and other methods, though, of catching players breaking his rules. We used to stay in a hotel on the West Coast where the rooms were separate bungalows. Logistically, it was a difficult layout to monitor, but ol' Charlie always had his ways to catch culprits breaking curfew. He would jam wax inside the key slot of the bungalows so you couldn't put your key in the door. If you went into the hotel office after hours saying you couldn't get into your room, he'd nail you that way. It would take the maintenance man to melt the wax so you could get into your room. Dressen would check the maintenance log in the morning.

How many times did I get caught? Not once. Remember, I was a young player when Charlie used to try that stuff. I couldn't afford to get caught.

Charlie was a feisty guy who put life back into the team. But he lost his own life while doing it. He died of a kidney infection after a heart attack during the 1966 season. I've never forgotten him, though.

Going for a Ride

As you probably know, the Tigers fly from city to city on their own plane now. They've done that for years. For one night in 1966, though, we also had our own fighter jet. It never left the ground, of course, and became more of a team prank than a team plane. But, man, did we have fun that night, and one of our esteemed teammates ended up in the cockpit while the plane was moving on the ground.

What actually happened was nothing close to anything I've ever seen reported over the years. The plane was not a model that had been hanging in the lobby. It was an actual P-40 from the hotel's parking lot. It also never ended up in the swimming pool, as I've seen written, nor did we ever dismantle or vandalize it.

Yes, several of the guys that night had too many "milk-shakes," as I often call cocktails, after a game in Anaheim, so it can be correctly construed they were up to some mischief. But they weren't being destructive. I know that for sure because I was there.

In the parking lot was a P-40, which had been flown by the Flying Tigers to defend China from the Japanese before the United States entered World War II. It was there because of a reunion those brave pilots were holding at our hotel. Trust me—the plane was the real thing, not a model, but I didn't disassemble it. So let me set the record perfectly straight. I did not take it apart. No one did. But the report that we were having fun at a party near the end of the season, well, that was correct.

The P-40 was a tail-dragging plane, so whoever was in the cockpit could control its direction on the ground. That night "whoever was in the cockpit" turned out to be a Detroit Tiger, not a Flying Tiger. But it was not Norm Cash, as you might expect. That's a good guess because Norm was a partier and a prankster, but he was at the back of the plane and not in the cockpit. In other words, he was behind the P-40, pushing it while a distinguished left-handed pitcher, whose last season with the team was 1967, was up in the cockpit.

I'm not telling you it was Hank Aguirre, but let the record show that we all loved Hank and that Hank liked to have fun. Anyway, with "a teammate" in the cockpit at the steering controls, Norm and the guys were pushing the plane across the hotel parking lot. They had it going at a pretty good clip when they suddenly pushed it over a curb, and the plane stopped short of the fence surrounding the swimming pool. I'm not sure why they had started pushing it, but I guess they felt it needed a new parking place. With the plane being as heavy as it was, however, it could not be pulled back over the curb. So that's where it was left.

Meanwhile, the culprits of this caper returned to the suite where we were drinking "our milkshakes." We knew it was only a matter of time before the phone would ring. When it did, Norm answered. The caller didn't identify himself, but he didn't have to. It was general manager Jim Campbell, and through the phone, we clearly heard the only two words he spoke. *"Move it!"*

The boss was not happy. So a bunch of guys went right back down to the parking lot and somehow put the plane back where they had found it. But that wasn't the last of it. Remember, taking place at the hotel was a reunion of the American pilots who helped defend China before our entry into World War II. All around the parking lot, befitting the reunion, were American and Chinese flags. Hmm, they sure looked like great souvenirs.

We flew home the next day from Anaheim on a commercial flight, and while we were waiting for our luggage, Campbell was standing nearby with manager Frank Skaff. Neither one was prepared for what he saw next. Our bags soon began to come off the conveyor belt. Here they came. The first one had a Chinese flag attached to it, the second one had an American flag, and then another Chinese flag, and so on.

Boys will be boys, after all, especially following a win on the road and during a team party. With permission and in return for whatever autographs and photos the pilots wanted, the guys had brought back some of the parking lot flags. Just a good old-fashioned baseball swap. But as I looked back after retrieving my luggage, there was Campbell, shaking his head in disbelief after seeing so many flags. I'll never forget that look. And I'm pretty sure he was mumbling something about "those damn ballplayers."

Don't Be Fooled by the Belly

Do I remember the base, the one and only that I stole? Of course I do.

So would you if—in 16 major league seasons—you never expected to steal any. But it wasn't just any base. I stole *third* base.

You know, I might have looked heavy—and for sure I had a belly on me—but I was a pretty good base runner. I wasn't fast, but I ran the bases well. I also ran them alertly. The Tigers even used me at times (five, to be exact) as a pinch-runner. I remember Charlie Dressen, our manager, being asked by reporters about it: "He runs better than you think he does," Charlie said. "And he knows how to slide. He knows several different slides, in fact: the fadeaway, the hook, the pop-up slide. He knows them all."

I had learned to slide early in my career. At some point, after all, pitchers get on base. Besides, the guy who signed me, Bernie DeViveiros, was our sliding coach when I was in the minors. So I thought it was important to at least pay attention.

One time in 1968, I ran for Eddie Mathews in a game against the Boston Red Sox. We were in first place but only two-and-a-half games ahead of the Cleveland Indians and Baltimore Orioles. We knew even then that we had a good team. But it was early June, and we weren't running away from the other teams yet. We went into the seventh inning down 4–1 at Fenway Park, but we were bouncing back like we did a lot of times that season.

We'd already chipped a run off the lead, and when Mathews singled Jim Price to third with one out, manager Mayo Smith sent me in as a pinch-runner for Mathews. It was a messy inning for the Red Sox. They made a couple of errors, threw a wild pitch, and walked a couple of guys. I went from first to second on a walk to Dick McAuliffe that loaded the bases, but I stayed at second when a wild pitch scored Price from third to make the score 4–3.

I don't recall why I didn't take third, but sometimes it pays to be cautious. Or overly patient, I suppose you could say. Either way, it paid off this time. When Rico Petrocelli, Boston's shortstop, threw away Mickey Stanley's ground ball for an error, I scored the tying run from second. With the ball not yet retrieved, McAuliffe scored behind me on the same play with what proved to be the winning run. Playing it safe at second on the wild pitch that scored Price hadn't cost us a run. More than that, it made my decision look like it had been the wise thing to do. Wise or not, that's why Mayo trusted my instincts as a runner. He knew I wouldn't take chances.

I wasn't a stranger to being on base, though. I'm not saying I was a good hitter, but I walked a lot. That's why my career on-base percentage (.215) was more than 100 points higher than my batting average (.110). Bottom line: I had more walks than hits in my career, so it was important for me to be a good base runner.

The base I stole happened in the home opener of the 1970 season against Cleveland. I was on second in a bunt situation with Cesar Gutierrez at the plate. When the Indians' third baseman Larry Brown charged in as Cesar squared around, it left third base open. I had taken my normal lead from second, but when I saw Brown moving in just as the pitcher was about to deliver, I remember thinking, *If he's going that way, I'm going this way.*

I actually slid into third, even though I was safe by 20 feet. Brown came back to the bag grumbling, "You just embarrassed me." I told him I wasn't trying to. I was just taking the base being given to me. "But I'm going to get my ass chewed out when I get back to the dugout," Brown said.

I told him I couldn't do anything about that, but he was right. I saw his manager vigorously talking to him later. When I was asked after the game how long had it been since I stole a base, I gave the reporters a smart ass answer: "1932, I think."

The fact of the matter was I used to steal bases left and right in amateur ball. When I started learning how to play baseball, I'd slide on the grass at the park near my house where there wasn't even a baseball diamond. I figured I needed to know the fundamentals if I was going to play this game.

So that time I stole third? As I said, I was safe by 20 feet. But I slid all the same.

Chapter 10

Game 4

"I'm mad as hell they even played it."

—pitcher Denny McLain

None of the other losses even came close. Game 4 was the absolute worst. In front of our own fans at Tiger Stadium, we lost 10–1, making almost as many errors (four) as we had hits (five). We'd gone into the game trying to convince ourselves that Bob Gibson was beatable, but we would not have beaten anyone playing the wretched way we did. Gibson was superb again, however, tossing his second complete game of the World Series. He didn't match the 17 strikeouts he had in the opener, but he reached double figures with 10.

Denny McLain didn't get out of the third inning. His 31-win magic was officially absent. A shadow of the pitcher he'd been in the regular season, Denny allowed four runs, three earned, on six hits in two and two-thirds innings. "He's obviously not at his best," observed the St. Louis Cardinals' Mike Shannon.

"I'm finished for the series," Denny told reporters after the game, even while manager Mayo Smith was saying he might be able to pitch again. "My shoulder is hurting me," Denny continued. "I doubt I can pitch again, but maybe they'll put a shot [of cortisone] in it. But I don't want an alibi. I got hit, period. I'm just not right."

McLain admitted to the *Detroit Free Press* that during a long rain delay in the third inning he asked Smith to take him out of the game. "I'm mad as hell they even played it," Denny said. "I didn't think they would start it. But I told Mayo [in the third] I just couldn't continue. I didn't want to take the chance of a long delay and then going out there with my arm tight. I don't want to hurt my arm because I have other seasons to think of."

As a sign of the beating to come, Lou Brock led off the game with a home run. For good measure Gibson also led off the Cardinals' fourth by reaching the seats against Joe Sparma. Struggling even more than McLain, Sparma and John Hiller combined to give up six runs in one-third of an inning.

Hitting .500 through four games and with seven stolen bases, Brock already appeared to be in the driver's seat of the new car that would be awarded to the World Series MVP. He also doubled and tripled as the Cardinals unleashed a 13-hit barrage against us that included seven extra-base hits: three doubles, two triples, and two home runs. What rankled us, though—not to the point of later knocking him down with a pitch but just remembering it for motivation—was that Brock stole third base in the eighth inning when the Cardinals led by nine runs. He had just emptied the bases with a three-run double. To some of our guys, that was the low point of the series, the moment at which the Cardinals were shoving our faces in it. Dick McAuliffe said it best: "That isn't the way the game should be played."

The lopsided loss put us down three games to one, and to many of our fans, it didn't look like we had a prayer of bouncing back after being outscored 17–4 in the last two games. We were a comeback team for sure—had been all year—but digging out of this hole was going to take some doing.

The only run we scored was Jim Northrup's home run in the fourth inning, but the fact that he hit the ball so hard off Gibson would prove to be worth remembering later in the series.

An indication of how little the home run meant at that time, however, occurred when vice president Hubert Humphrey came to our clubhouse after the game and said "congratulations" to Northrup. "For what?" Jim replied.

An eerie parallel was the fact that I had drawn a bases-loaded walk and hit a home run in Game 2—only to have Gibson answer with the same combination in Game 4. In addition to connecting off Sparma, he drew a bases-loaded walk off Hiller in the eighth, after which Brock doubled, of course.

The Cardinals not only were proving they could do it all, but they also *were* doing it all. To make matters worse, this was the Sunday game of the World Series—the telecast that would attract the largest television audience. Before it became a rout anyway. As Jerry Green of *The Detroit News* put it: "This was supposed to be baseball's Super Sunday." It turned out to be baseball's sloppy Sunday instead.

Rain delayed the start for 37 minutes and then returned in the third to delay the game another 74 minutes. It was at that point that it became ridiculous. With a 4–0 lead, the Cardinals were naturally eager to see it last long enough to become official. So they ran themselves into intentional outs while we stalled as much as we could, hoping for heavier rain. When Julian Javier tried to steal second in the fifth as our pitcher Daryl Patterson was holding the ball, umpire Bill Kinnamon told Cardinals manager Red Schoendienst that "It did not look good."

Bob Talbert, a columnist for the *Free Press* known for his humor, wrote that "It was the first World Series game in which rust was a major factor." Green suggested the World Series had become a "farce" because of how the two teams behaved once the possibility of a shortened game became real.

Even the umpires were upset at the mess the game became because it had not been their decision to play. That ruling came from the commissioner's office. "Whenever they want a whipping boy, they hang it on us," umpire Stan Landes told reporters after the game in the umpires' room. "For 162 games a year—rain or shine—we're permitted to make the call. Then along comes the World Series, and they take it away from us. We have the guts to make the decisions. What we need is the authority."

Rain or no rain, though, we played a terrible game. Al Kaline called it the worst we had played all year and "one of the worst in the 14 years I've been with the team."

When it was over, all we could do was grasp at whatever straws of hope we could find. For instance, there was the glimmer of a chance that if somehow we could extend the World Series to a seventh game, we might not find Gibson so overpowering. "My arm is tired," the Cardinals ace had said. "I hope we end it tomorrow."

Game 7 wasn't the immediate problem, though. The urgent need to play better was. There wouldn't even be a Game 6 if we didn't get past Game 5. And I would be the one staring at the pressure.

More than 2,500 stores in the Detroit area were looted or burned during the riots of 1967. Another 400 buildings had to be demolished because of extensive damage. (AP Images)

A man is taken into custody during the riots in Detroit on July 23, 1967. Authorities made more than 7,000 arrests. (AP Images)

Police patrol a section of Detroit near 12ᵗʰ Street during the riots, which left a reported 43 people dead and nearly 1,200 injured. (AP Images)

An active duty member of the Air National Guard, I was called in to help with the Detroit riots during the summer of 1967. (AP Images)

Using Al Kaline's thin-handled bat, I hit the only home run of my major league career during the third inning of Game 2 of the 1968 World Series. (AP Images)

I deliver a pitch during my six-hit, one-run, complete-game victory in Game 2 of the 1968 World Series. (AP Images)

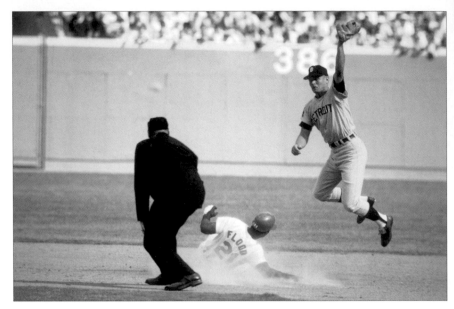

A superb base runner, St. Louis Cardinals outfielder Curt Flood beats a throw to Mickey Stanley, who was inserted as our starting shortstop so we could keep Al Kaline's powerful bat in the lineup. (USA TODAY Sports Images)

First baseman Norm Cash, who hit .385 during the 1968 World Series, heads to first base. (USA TODAY Sports Images)

In a controversial call, Tigers catcher Bill Freehan tags out speedy Lou Brock, who was racing home from second base during the fifth inning of Game 5. My view of it was great, and I know that Brock never touched the plate. (AP Images)

In a favorite photo of mine, my daughter Kimberly kisses me after I won Game 5 of the 1968 World Series. (Mickey Lolich)

I embrace catcher Bill Freehan after throwing a five-hit complete game to win Game 7 of the 1968 World Series. (AP Images)

The MVP of the 1968 World Series after winning three games, I pour out champagne during the postgame celebration. (AP Images)

From left to right, my three daughters—Kimberly (who was eight years old at the time), Jody (three years old), and Stacy (five years old)—hang out with me at Tiger Stadium. (Mickey Lolich)

I used to infuriate Tigers general manager Jim Campbell by riding my motorcycle to Tiger Stadium. (Mickey Lolich)

My daughter Kimberly recognizes me as a starting pitcher of the Detroit Tigers. (Mickey Lolich)

*I hold my daughter, Kimberly, with my wife, Joyce, during a trip to Oregon, where I grew up. (*The Oregonian*)*

My wife, Joyce, remains by my side, including during Detroit Tigers Fantasy Camp in 2018. (Rick Dupler)

Chapter 11

Rules, Rides, and Runs

"I wish he'd gone into the doughnut business 10 years earlier."
—Hall of Fame outfielder Reggie Jackson

I never believed in scouting reports on hitters. Even if they were available, I didn't pay attention to them. None of that preparation stuff meant anything to me, including pregame meetings to go over the hitters we were about to face. I walked out of some of them but wanted to walk out of most. I know what takes place in today's baseball, though. There are meetings for this, meetings for that. So much more information is available to a pitcher now that wasn't available in my day.

Know what though? I'd still pitch the way I did. My approach was to go with what was working for me—simple as that. If I went down to the bullpen to warm up for a game and I'm throwing a fastball that's echoing in the ballpark because it is popping the catcher's glove so hard—and if I have a mediocre curveball at the same time—my best pitch when I step on the mound was going to be my fastball. Never mind the so-called scouting reports. Now let's say you're a first-ball, fastball hitter. Fine, I'm throwing my fastball. Here it comes, baby. See if you can hit it. That's the way it was with me against most hitters I faced, including the best in the business. I'd challenge them. I'd dare them to hit it.

They would be looking for a first-pitch breaking ball because that's what they would get from other lefties. But I would pound the best sluggers of their day—guys like Reggie Jackson, Carl Yastrzemski, Boog Powell—with fastballs. It was to my added advantage that they hit left-handed. Yaz fanned more against me than he did against any other pitcher. I struck him out 35 times. Nobody else stuck him out more than 22 times. Yaz hit seven home runs off me, but I held him to a .226 batting average. Only one left-hander (Jim Kaat) struck Reggie out more than I did, but I think we both frustrated him. "Mickey Lolich was no crafty left-hander," Jackson said in an interview with Bill Dow, a freelance writer in Detroit. "He had a fastball that would knock your dick off. Plus he wasn't some guy looking to go five, six, or seven innings. He went nine—and he never missed a start, at least not against me he didn't. Every time we played Detroit, I had to face the son of a bitch. Mickey was a gallon of ice cream when you only wanted a cone. He was a great pitcher. I wish he had gone into the doughnut business 10 years earlier."

As for Boog, he never could figure me out. I remember him saying, "Damn you, Mickey, when are going to throw me a breaking ball?" Boog hit .178 against me but got a measure of revenge with a long first-inning home run in 1970 that he must have enjoyed.

I wasn't effective against these great hitters, though, because of scouting reports. I was effective because I wasn't afraid to challenge them. Nowadays, they'd say, "Oh, don't throw him a fastball. He'll hit a fastball." All you're doing is putting a negative thought in my mind when you say that—as if the hitter would always win the showdown. I say you need to show more confidence than that.

When we had a meeting before the World Series, they called all the pitchers together and started going through the St. Louis batting order. I don't remember the exact scouting report on Lou Brock, for instance, but it would have been something like: "Don't pitch him inside. Pitch him away." So I got up and walked out of the room. "What the hell is he doing? Go get him," said manager Mayo Smith, who sent pitching coach Johnny Sain after me.

"Mickey, you have to be in here for the pitchers' meeting," Sain said.

"No," I said. "I don't want to hear about what not to throw a hitter. It's all negative. 'Don't throw this guy this pitch. Don't throw him that pitch. You can only pitch him this way.' I couldn't stand it."

All pitching comes down to me and you, the pitcher against the hitter. Here it comes. If I was throwing fastballs, you'd be getting the best I have—and I'd be trying to throw it for a strike. If I was going to be throwing curveballs, I'd be trying to throw the best curve I had for a strike. I also never bounced one on purpose to see if a hitter would chase it. I didn't pitch that way.

And these catchers who supposedly call a great game—that's all I ever hear about some guys. Let me tell you something, when a hitter came up to the plate, I'd always know who he was and what kind of stuff I had that night. So I knew what the first three pitches to him would be. What I'm saying is that I called my own game all the time. The catcher, even one as great as Bill Freehan, didn't have to do much. If I moved my head at all—even with a little twitch as Freehan was staring out at me—he would know I didn't like the sign and that the pitch he called for wasn't getting thrown.

I also didn't want my catchers setting up all over the place the way some of them do today. Intended pitch locations and selection can be detected way too easily. And if detected, there'd always be a way of conveying that info to the hitter. For instance, if an opposing coach at third base called out your uniform number as part of his chatter, it would mean he thought you were throwing a breaking ball. If he didn't say your number, he thought it would be a fastball. That's how a coach could convey his thoughts to the hitter. It worked the same way for locations. If he thought the pitch might be away, a coach would yell your first name. Calling out your last name would mean the pitch was going to be inside. And the way your catcher set up could give a ton away. But you didn't give anything away if your catcher always set up in the same place, like just off the outside corner. It wasn't always easy for catchers to catch me. You had to be athletic. Freehan caught the vast majority of my games and he was very athletic. He also was consistent in his set-up.

This isn't about it all being "better back then." But there are some catchers today I wouldn't throw to. I'd refuse. Think I'm kidding? Yeah, so did those who didn't believe I'd refuse to go to meetings.

A Lesson in Awkwardness

One day in Minneapolis, I was sitting in the hotel lobby not doing much when Bill Freehan came walking by. We said hello to each other, and then he said, "I'm going shopping."

With time on my hands before a night game, I answered, "Where ya going?"

He replied, "Bloomingdale's."

When I asked if I could come along, Bill said, "Sure, c'mon."

So we walked over to the store and took the escalator up a floor. I wasn't sure where we were going. I was just tagging along, but suddenly there we were in the lingerie department.

I thought that maybe Bill was buying something for his wife. But I already felt out of place. I mean, here I am walking around with him—one of my good friends on the team—when suddenly he heads to the bra department. I trailed behind him but really wasn't sure what he was up to.

A salesperson came over. I think she was summer help because she couldn't have been more than 17 and asked Freehan if she could be of assistance. "I'd like to see some falsies," Freehan said.

What? Now I really had no clue what he was doing. His reply stunned the young sales associate, who quickly said, "Sir, please, you're older than I am. I don't want to be harassed. And if you do harass me, I'll have to call for security."

You could clearly see she was nervous with what Bill had said to her. Meanwhile, I had already taken three or four steps backward from the counter because I didn't want any part of whatever was about to happen. I still didn't know what Bill was up to. Aware of the strange situation in which he put the girl, though, and now knowing she didn't trust him, Bill quickly said, "No, no, no, you don't understand. I'm a professional baseball player with the Detroit Tigers and…"

"I don't care who you work for," she replied, interrupting him before he could even begin.

"I need to explain something to you," Freehan said. "I'm a catcher."

"So what?" She answered.

"This guy behind me," Bill said, referring to me, "throws hard, and his balls are heavy." That explanation didn't help. "I mean his fastball is very heavy when it hits my glove," Bill explained, still trying to get out of the mess he'd made for himself but only digging a deeper hole. "It hurts my hand," he added, going through a squeezing motion with his fingers extended. That didn't help, either.

"I need you to walk away from here right now," the girl said.

"No, please, let me explain this to you," Freehan replied. "I take a falsie, wrap it in tape, and slide it into my glove. Because it's made out of foam rubber, it gives me a cushion against heavy pitches. A falsie is the perfect shape."

With a look of disbelief, meaning she still didn't know if Bill was crazy or not, she then turned to me and asked, "Is he telling the truth?"

Instead of the three to four steps I'd taken back, I had now taken five or six. I was also thinking that she had already pushed a button underneath the counter, the store detective was going to show up, and we were going to be escorted out or arrested at any minute.

But then the tide turned. Beginning to believe him a little, she asked Bill what size he needed. As a visual reply, he held up his hand in a squeezing motion again—as if he was some kind of ventriloquist attempting to speak through his fingers. "You know, you're a real smart ass," she said.

"I need one that fits in the palm of my hand," Bill said. At that point, she reached under the counter to pull out some different sizes. Being thorough, he put his hand on each one before finally choosing the right size.

The young clerk never did laugh, though. She never even smiled. She was uncomfortable all the way through the conversation, but she finally realized Bill was serious. She told him the price, the transaction was completed, and we started to walk out. But I had to tell him, "You know, Bill, if you had told me what you were going to buy, I might have stayed in the lobby."

In fact, I know I would have. "You kind of creeped me out," I said. "I thought we were going to end up in jail." After that, I'm happy to say, Bill's wife did his shopping for him. That's what I heard anyway.

A Rare Missed Start

I don't claim it, but others have on my behalf. They say I was blessed with legendary durability—and that my capacity to bounce back was pretty impressive as well. For instance, I recovered from the only game in which I was ever hurt with a 16-strikeout performance to tie my own team record. It hadn't exactly been a long-standing mark, though. I had also struck out 16 in the game before I got hurt.

So after setting the record but getting hit on the arm by a line drive in my next start, I merely picked up where I left off. In any event it was one of the most memorable sequences in my career. Here's the way it unfolded.

On May 23, 1969, at Tiger Stadium and with the previous strikeout record holder Paul Foytack in attendance (because he had thrown batting practice for us that day), I managed to strike out 16 California Angels, including power hitter Dick Stuart four times. Neither one of us—myself nor catcher Bill Freehan—knew what was at stake, though, until Stuart came up for his final at-bat with one out in the ninth.

Sometimes you are so focused on pitching that you're oblivious to the details of the game. To me the number of strikeouts I had was an incidental detail. When I got two strikes on

Stuart, though, I could hear a murmur go through the crowd. I knew something was going on but didn't know what. I thought maybe Stuart had never struck out four times in a game before. He had—several times, in fact—so it wasn't his situation that was causing the stir. It was mine. One more strikeout would give me 16, a Tigers record. Call me clueless, but its immediate impact—beyond getting us to within one out of a victory—was lost on me. I didn't know I was on the brink of a milestone.

When I fanned Stuart for the fourth time, I thought I had maybe 11 or 12 strikeouts. I only knew it was more than 10. Even after the final out, I didn't realize what was going on. Neither did Freehan. We soon found out, though. I had pitched my way into the Tigers' record book, and while most records eventually get broken, it wasn't until 2013 that Anibal Sanchez broke my mark with 17 K's against the Atlanta Braves. My record stood for 44 years.

I wasn't smiling when I left the mound in my next start, though. I was wincing. On May 27, en route to taking a 4–3 loss in Oakland to the A's, Danny Cater's line drive hit me just below my left elbow. Bruised, in pain, and encountering some inflammation, I was sent home by the Tigers, who feared I might miss several starts. I was scheduled to pitch four days later in Seattle, but manager Mayo Smith said, "No, go home for treatment instead."

So the start I missed was in Seattle against the Pilots. (They weren't the Mariners yet.)

Once I got home, my arm was still very sore, so it really looked like I would miss more than one start. But when I tested my arm and my tolerance for the discomfort two days later, I found I could start after all. "Besides," I told the media, "your body tells you when it's time to pitch."

It didn't appear to be a wise decision to come back that soon when Seattle's Dick Simpson hit my first pitch at Tiger Stadium for a home run. But by the end of the seventh inning, I had 16 strikeouts again, tying the record I set two starts ago. I was in position to easily break my own mark, but the K-parade suddenly ended, which is why you never count your chickens. Or your strikeouts.

I pitched through the ninth inning. Pat Dobson took the loss in the 10th. But of the final six outs I was on the mound for, four were ground-outs, and two were pop-ups. Having a chance through the seventh to end up with as many as 22 strikeouts, I stalled at 16. But I believe the game was described in the papers the next day as a masterpiece, though to me any game your team loses can't be labeled as such.

But I bounced back to win my next five decisions and eight of my next nine. And by July 24, my record was 14–2. We tried our best to bring more joy to Tigertown in 1969, but it did not turn out to be another World Series season for us. Unfortunately, I never pitched in another.

Easy Rider

I used to infuriate the Tigers by riding my motorcycle to work—meaning, of course, to Tiger Stadium. Man, were they pissed. I'd wear a helmet, but general manager Jim Campbell, the big boss, was certain that something terrible was going to happen to me on the long rides to or from my house. So he tried to tell me I was forbidden to ride the bike, but I wouldn't agree to the ban except on the days I was starting.

It wasn't the first time I had run into objections. My mom and dad weren't happy when I bought my first motorcycle at age 18. But that's because they thought I was too young. And to their credit, they didn't freak out about my love of riding as much as the Tigers did years later.

The first day I rode my bike to Tiger Stadium was in 1966. But the second day was more eventful. When I arrived, I took my helmet off and started walking past the security station as usual. This time, though, the guard stopped me and said, "Mr. Campbell wants to see you."

Somehow he already knew about—and was objecting to—my mode of transportation. I'd been around long enough already to know that when Campbell wanted to see you, he meant *now*. So right away, I went upstairs and walked into his office—that long office of his where he'd sit at the far end. I figured I was in for a quarrel. I had hardly taken a step before he told me to "Shut the damn door!"

When I shut the door, the next thing he demanded was for me to get my ass onto the chair in front of his desk. Then all of a sudden, he started ranting, raving, and cussing at me about my motorcycle. "Stay off the damn bike, Mickey!" He demanded.

"I'm not going to do it," I replied.

"What do you mean you're not going to do it?" He bellowed. "I'm your boss and I'm telling you to stay off that bike."

He really didn't like when I next said, "Jim, it's not in my contract that I can't ride it."

"I don't give a damn," said Campbell, huffing and puffing. "I'm telling you never to ride that thing again."

By then, we were going back and forth pretty actively. "I'm going to keep riding it," I told him again.

"Then I'll put it in your contract for next year that you can't," he said. "In that case I won't sign," I fired back. As one of the Tigers' starting pitchers—an important piece of their puzzle—I felt I had some leverage but not much. We kept going at it until at the end in a friendlier tone, Campbell asked me, "How long have you been riding?"

I told him since I was 18 and that I used to race bikes back in Portland. "What? You used to *race* motorcycles?" Campbell said with more bluster than ever at what he was hearing.

"All the time through the mountains and hills," I told him, "but not around a track. They were cross-country bikes. I'm primarily a dirt bike rider. But I do have a street bike Kawasaki gave me that I ride only to the ballpark."

"Which way do you come from home?" Campbell wanted to know.

"On the expressways," I told him.

"You're going to get killed out there," he replied.

I said it was a lot safer to ride on expressways than on city streets, where people constantly run stop signs and red lights and where other drivers pull out in front of you from a parking place. "The streets are more dangerous," I told him. "On the freeways you're safer. You're going faster, but you're safer."

Having met his match, Campbell finally realized he wasn't going to stop me from riding. He tried hard but didn't win the debate. So when I finally got up to leave, he didn't say anything more until I was almost gone. Then he yelled at me from the other end of his office. "I rode motorcycles for two years in the service," he said. "They are a lot of fun, aren't they? Be safe."

Imagine that. As much as Campbell, a worrier from way back, didn't want me riding, it turned out that he also loved bikes. With that, our discussion ended. The subject never again came up between us. He left it alone. And so did I.

Riding to Shea Stadium after I got traded to the New York Mets in 1975 was entirely different. I remember the first time I rode to the ballpark there, Tom Seaver was in the parking lot at the time. As we walked together to the clubhouse, he said he couldn't believe I'd ridden a motorcycle. "Why?" I asked. "I always did in Detroit."

"Because there are tons of fans at the gate here after a game wanting us to stop and sign—or just to talk," Seaver said. "How in the hell are you ever going to get past them on a motorcycle? The people will never get out of your way. They might even pull you right off your bike."

What Seaver didn't know is that I had already made my departure plans. I told the guard at Shea I'd be parking underneath the stadium. That's where I would fire up my bike before leaving. "Then I'm going to rap my pipes three times real loud," I said. "When you hear that, all the fans at the gate are going to hear it, too, because the sound will be bouncing off concrete in the tunnel. I'll get my speed up and take a right-hand turn out of the ballpark. You watch: the crowd will open up like Moses parting the Red Sea."

Seaver said he wanted to see the plan in action firsthand, so it didn't take many games before he was out there to watch me leave. It worked exactly as I told him it would. After hearing that bike, the people scattered. "Hey, Mickey, tell me where to get a motorcycle, too," Seaver said. "I want to leave the way you do." I think his intentions were good, but I don't believe he ever bought one.

What I didn't know until later was how dangerous the area was that I drove through to and from Shea. Its nickname was Fort Apache. When my teammates found out I was leaving on a bike late at night and what my route was, they said, "You're crazy, that's the meanest, nastiest part of New York. They're always shooting at cars out there."

If their warnings were meant to scare me, they failed. "I guess I better hunker down on the tank pretty low then," I said. "That'll give them a smaller target."

Nothing ever got me off my bike, as it turned out. Not the way Campbell reacted when I was a Tiger, nor the alarm with which my teammates reacted when I was with the Mets. I just kept on riding.

Chapter 12

Game 5

"We couldn't lose all three games at home."

—outfielder Al Kaline

Despite the feeling there was no way it could, our situation got worse before it got better.

We were down 3–1 in the World Series. We'd been outscored 17–2 in the last 14 innings.

To be honest, we hadn't done anything well since Game 2. And as if all that wasn't a steep enough hill for us to climb, here I was trying to warm up in the bullpen for Game 5 when a rare rendition of our national anthem was about to be sung.

I heard later that CBS was flooded with complaints about it as was the local channel in Detroit that was showing the game. But nobody had the same reason for disliking it that I did.

Nothing against Jose Feliciano, who sang it, but it seemed to me that his version of the anthem took forever to sing—as well as forever to end. I just stood there, and stood there, and stood there.

In the midst of working up a sweat for the start I was about to make in what could be an elimination game for us, I was cooling down. Worse than that, when the anthem was finally over, the third-base umpire told me I didn't have much time before I needed to head to the mound.

Not much time?

I could not believe it. I hadn't even thrown a breaking ball yet before I was told the schedule had changed because of national television. My entire routine was screwed up. So all I really had going for me when the game began was a fastball, which wasn't all that fast yet. I would need the entire first inning to get up to game speed, and the St. Louis Cardinals seemed to know that. At least Lou Brock did.

In Game 2 Brock had been mortal enough to look at a called third strike from me in the first inning. But he came into Game 5 on a tear. He was 6-for-his-last-9—only to make it 7-for-10 by leading off with a double. One out later Curt Flood singled him in, and, voila, I'd already allowed a run. That's when Orlando Cepeda stepped in. For years I would remember the 3–2 pitch I threw Cepeda as a nothing fastball that he jumped all over. Wow, was I wrong. When I saw the pitch again on a replay of Game 5, I said, "Oh my God, it was a breaking ball."

It was a better pitch than I remember it being, but not a good one. With Flood on, Cepeda hit it into the left-field seats at Tiger Stadium to give the Cardinals a 3–0 lead—a potential disaster that I attributed, and still do, to not having enough time to warm up. I mean, all of a sudden, it had been game time, and I wasn't ready.

By the end of their first inning, I felt better about the pitches I was throwing, especially when Tim McCarver took a called third strike. But I didn't know if the Cardinals had already done enough damage to win the game—and, consequently, the World Series.

I can assure you it was not a good feeling.

Nelson Briles, whom we beat in Game 2, looked sharper this time. Headed into the bottom of the fourth, the Cardinals still had a three-run lead. I had settled down, but we'd done nothing at the plate against Briles. In short, we were in deep trouble, but I couldn't afford to think we were. When I used to speak on the banquet tour, I'd say to Tigers fans about our predicament, "I thought I'd give up three runs in the top of the first just to scare the shit out of all you people."

Two bright spots were that the Cardinals hadn't added to their lead since the first inning—and that we finally prevented Brock from stealing second in the third, when Bill Freehan threw him out on a pitchout. That was a triumph in itself. But it would not be the most important play of the game involving Brock. Not by a long shot.

Meanwhile, it was my job—while we hunted and pecked for runs—to limit the Cards so we could stage a comeback. It wasn't always easy to do so, however, such as in the fourth when Mike Shannon ended up at second on a one-out error by Norm Cash—our ninth error in the first five games. Most of the blunders had been costly. In our three losses, we had made seven errors. The Cardinals had made only one. Then again, they had played well thus far. We had not.

Following Shannon in the fourth, McCarver made it more of a one-out jam for me with a walk, but Ron Davis flied out to center, and Dal Maxvill took a called third strike. As much as the top of the Cardinals' batting order pestered us the entire series, the bottom of their order struggled. The trio of Davis, Maxvill, and Roger Maris went 3-for-48.

Although I struck out Maxvill to get out of that jam, I really wasn't pitching that well. I was up instead of down, not hitting the corners often enough. For instance, the last pitch to Maxvill was a bad breaking ball. It wasn't down. He should have hit the crap out of it, but I got away with it.

With the clock ticking, the first sign of hope for us offensively was Mickey Stanley's leadoff triple in our half of the fourth. While trying to get out of the way of a pitch, Al Kaline tapped the ball back to Briles for the first out. Cash followed with a sacrifice fly.

We now trailed 3–1, but at least we were on the scoreboard. From where I was in the tunnel, smoking my Tareyton cigarette and having a Pepsi, I could tell from the sound of worried Tigers fans that we'd just done something good. But one run was only a start.

Still in the fourth, Willie Horton followed with a triple to right-center. I love watching the replay of this hit because Willie was so aggressive in heading for third. With a headfirst slide, he beat the throw—barely beat it—but it was a gamble for him to even try. We all were thinking, *If we can score here, we're back in this game.* Smart or not, Willie's triple was a huge play because what happened next, in my opinion, was the turning point of the World Series. I've always thought that.

With Horton on third, two outs, and us down 3–1, we got a big break. Jim Northrup hit a grounder directly to Julian Javier at second that looked entirely routine—until it wasn't. Something, maybe just a stone, made the ball hop over Javier's head for a single that drove in Willie. "We were fine until then," Briles said.

From that point on, thankfully everything started going downhill for the Cardinals. Plus the bad-hop run Horton scored on was instrumental in keeping me in the game. If the score had remained 3–1, I probably would have been pinch-hit for in the fifth, my next time up. I probably would have been. Instead, we were only a run down when my at-bat came around.

So manager Mayo Smith rode the rapids with me. The play that almost everyone else thinks was the turning point, though, took place in the top of the fifth and still is one of the most talked about World Series moments of all time. Naturally, it involved Brock, who doubled with one out. I saw him that winter at a dinner where he asked me, "How did they advise you to throw to me?" I told him the plan was to pitch him away. "I loved being pitched away," he said. "I don't know why teams tried to do it."

At that point, hands down, he was the odds-on MVP of the series. He had to be. But it was on Javier's single to left with Brock on second that the famous play, which is talked about even now, took place. Trying to score on Javier's hit, Brock did not slide at home. Not only that, we executed the play perfectly.

Willie made a great throw, Freehan blocked the plate in a way that catchers aren't allowed to anymore, and Brock's foot—though he's always argued otherwise—never touched the plate. Umpire Doug Harvey called him out because he was. I was right there. My view of it was the best of anyone's. Brock's foot never touched home plate.

I think he knew that because after his momentum took him past the plate and the call had been made, he went back to touch it. This is what I've always said and what I've heard my teammates say about the play as well: if you touched the plate the first time, Lou, why did you go back and touch it again? Through the years, it's been a strong argument on our behalf. "That play lifted us," Freehan said. "You could feel it."

But it didn't put us ahead. We were down 3–2 when I struck out against Briles in the fifth. I was still in the game, though, and finally throwing some good pitches. We had a chance in the sixth when we loaded the bases with two outs. Freehan grounded out to short, however. He struggled at the plate the entire series. Freehan and I are good friends, and when we would appear together at the various functions, he'd kid me about this or that, the way ballplayers do. My comeback would always be, "Yeah, but I got one more hit than you did in the World Series."

It was true. I ended up with three hits to Freehan's two. But he always took the teasing the right way. "You might have gotten more hits, but we cashed the same check," he'd often say to me.

So much of the attention on offense in those seven games went to Brock—and rightly so.

We had guys who had good World Series, too. Kaline had 11 hits and Cash had 10, but my word, Brock had 13 hits, six of which went for extra bases—three doubles, a triple, and two home runs.

He also scored six runs, drove in five, and stole seven bases. We didn't have a stolen base the entire series, but speed wasn't our forte. It was the essence of the Cardinals' offense, though, and true to their makeup, they were speedily closing in on winning the World Series.

In fact, they were only eight outs away after Briles struck out Don Wert to start the bottom of the seventh. My turn to bat was next, but I didn't expect it to happen. Thinking he was going to pinch hit for me, Gates Brown had gone to the bat rack as soon as the inning began.

But if he was planning to take me out while Wert was up, Mayo hadn't told anyone yet.

Smith had done some things that season that not only surprised and confused me, but one of them downright pissed me off. I'm talking about when he took me out of the starting rotation in early August. There was a stretch of five starts that year in which I was 0–3 with an ugly ERA, so he came out to where I was shagging balls in the outfield one evening and told me about his plan to put me in the bullpen. I was not happy with it, to say the least, and I told him so. "You're going to need me," I told him as I walked away.

I wasn't out of the rotation long, just a few weeks, but the Tigers were happy with how my relief appearances turned out. And so was I. In a stretch of 10 games, I was the winning pitcher in four of them. Then they put me back in the rotation, and I won two more before the end of August. I was rebounding at just the right time.

After losing my first start in September, I went 4–0 with a 1.45 ERA in my next four starts. By the time the World Series rolled around, I was pitching the best I had all year. By Game 5 Mayo not only fully trusted me, but he also wasn't afraid to show it. Any number of times with us hanging on by a thread, he could have yanked me, and the fans would've understood why.

With us trailing 3–0, he could have used a pinch-hitter for me in the third inning when I came up to bat for the first time. He could have done the same thing in the fifth when time was beginning to run out. Mayo also could have called for a right-hander from the bullpen when Cepeda came up to hit in the top of the eighth as the potential tying run. It had been Cepeda, after all, who'd connected off me in the first. And twice in the ninth, there were opportunities for Smith to take me out if it looked to him like I was tiring. The first was when McCarver led off with a single, bringing the potential tying run to the plate. The second chance was when pinch-hitter Ed Spiezio capped an extended at-bat with a single to left after fouling off seven pitches. McCarver took second on the play. Another manager might have called for a fresh pitcher after Spiezio's great at-bat with one out. Mayo stayed the course, though. He stuck with me to finish it, which I did by striking out Maris and getting Brock, of all people, to hit a game-ending chopper back to the mound.

The point at which Smith gambled the most with me, however, was in the seventh when my turn to bat came around with one out, the bases empty, and us still down by a run. Wert had struck out for the first out, and when I looked around to see who was pinch-hitting for me, no one was. Only eight outs away from possibly losing the World Series, Mayo was leaving me in. "I defied the experts by letting Mickey bat," he said with a smile later. "It was the seventh inning, so we had two more shots at it if it didn't work. If Wert had gotten on leading off, I would have hit for Lolich, but with one out and nobody on, I felt it wasn't a gamble. [Making hard decisions] is what we're paid to do."

It wasn't Smith's hunch that I would jump-start the offense. Oh no, it was his hunch that the Cardinals wouldn't tack on runs as long as I stayed in the game. That's how much faith Mayo had in me—or how little he trusted our bullpen at the time. "I don't blame him if he didn't trust us," said John Hiller, who turned into a great relief pitcher but wasn't one yet. "We hadn't done much right."

The incredible bonus of it all was that I responded with a single. I hit a little flare to right-center field, at which I yelled, "Get down, you son of a bitch, get down" the entire time I was running to first. "Mickey is becoming some kind of hitter," Kaline joked later. "But maybe I should take some credit for it. He's been using my bats."

Davis dove for the ball in right, but it hit the ground in front of his glove. Suddenly, as the tying run, I was on base with one out, giving the manager yet another chance to take me out. At least that's how it must have looked. I knew that Mayo wasn't going to pinch run for me, though. Heck no, he still wanted me on the mound. That's why he let me hit in the first place. Besides, he gave me more credit than most as a runner—albeit a runner who had gained weight.

At times I would poke fun at the pounds I had added as a Tiger. They still listed me at 185 when I really weighed at least 215. I once said that I would "tilt the field" when I ran. But the fact is, I still thought of myself as a decent runner. In any case, since I was at first base and staying in the game, I was the guy who was going to score the tying run in the bottom of the seventh. However, a more solid hit than my dinky little leadoff single was likely needed for that to happen.

Dick McAuliffe followed my hit with a single to right that moved me to second, though my big turn there, as if I had thoughts of taking third, raised some eyebrows. What really helped was that after Joe Hoerner pulled ahead of Stanley with a 1–2 count, he walked him to load the bases. Now we had Kaline at the plate—a scenario that was a storyteller's dream. It was to keep Kaline's bat in the lineup that Mayo did all of his Stanley-to-shortstop maneuvering for the series, and now Kaline was facing a golden opportunity for that strategy to pay off.

Al swung and missed Hoerner's first pitch. The crowd at Tiger Stadium groaned. We still trailed, mind you. But on the next pitch, a fastball that might have missed the outside corner had he let it go, Kaline dropped a two-run single into right-center. Not one to show emotion in front of an opponent, Kaline stood calmly at first as if he had singled with the bases empty instead of giving us a late 4–3 lead in a game we had to win. "It wasn't one of the harder balls I've ever hit," Kaline said later, "but it was one of the sweetest. We just couldn't lose all three games at home. We couldn't let the fans down like that. I'd been embarrassed by the way we had played. My pride was hurt. People watching must have thought we were a bad team, but I knew we weren't."

Before he exited, Hoerner allowed another hit, Cash's single to right on which Stanley scored. We were finally getting some timely hits. So it was a 5–3 lead that I took into the top of the eighth. It was my job to preserve it, though, and to do that, I needed some defensive help. As I said, we were finally playing good baseball, and that certainly included McAuliffe's great play in the eighth to keep Flood's ground ball from going through to center with a runner already on first.

Ray Oyler, who had taken over at short when we took the lead, was upended by a sliding Javier on McAuliffe's toss to second base. But we got the out. Mayo called it the unsung play of the game. "It might have been game over if Mac doesn't make that play," he said.

Instead of two runners on and no outs, the Cardinals had a runner on first with one out. I had allowed a home run on a curveball to Cepeda in the first, so I threw him fastballs after that. He popped one up to right for the second out of the eighth. Fortunately, my fastball was better late in the game than early, and I got Shannon swinging at one to end the eighth.

Spiezio's one-out at-bat in the ninth after McCarver's lead-off single was an ordeal. It felt like I pitched an entire ballgame just against him. But bearing down against a hitter I had a history of doing well against, I got Maris out on curves for the second out after Spiezio's single.

That brought up Brock. Hollywood couldn't have scripted it better.

I was wary of Lou's power. He had shown me more of it than I ever thought he had, so you can only imagine how happy I was to get a tapper hit back to me for the game's final out.

When Brock had come up in the ninth, I thought *If there's one time to get him out, dear God let it be now.*

What I also loved about that game is that my two-year-old daughter Kimberly gave me a big kiss after the last out, a photo that appeared on the front page of the Detroit newspapers the next day. To this day, it is one of my favorite photos ever.

But we had done what we needed to do against the Cardinals. We had forced a Game 6 to be played in St. Louis. It wasn't an official comeback yet, but it wouldn't take much more to become one.

Chapter 13

Who We Were

"There was a special chemistry."

—infielder Tommy Matchick

It's been a long time since 1968, so we have lost some of the players who were on that Tigers team. Ballplayers aren't immune to the aging process. I wish we were, but we aren't.

Knees had to be replaced. Aches became pains. We've also done our share of forgetting.

And every time we lose a teammate, I think of him as the carefree athlete he once was, playing a game for a living and playing it well.

We got along like brothers on the Tigers in 1968. Most of us did, and most of us lived by the same rules. To have good teammates, you have to be one. After all, like all baseball teams, we spent more time together than we did with our families. It was counterproductive not to get along with each other. But with this Tigers team from top to bottom, as our friend Tommy Matchick once said, there was a special chemistry.

I have fond memories of my teammates from that championship season. Some of them remain my friends to this day. Some I haven't seen in years. Others I will never see again. It was an honor, though, to play with them. It was an honor to win with them. So let the roll call of yesteryear begin. This was the class of 1968.

Position Players

BILL FREEHAN, catcher—No catcher/starter combination ever teamed up for more games than Bill and I did. I made 459 starts for the Tigers. Bill caught 324 of them. The Boston/Milwaukee Braves' tandem of Warren Spahn and Del Crandall ranks second with 316.

Somewhere down the list, but still impressive, are the 207 Jack Morris starts that Lance Parrish caught. Bill knew what pitches I wanted to throw in almost every situation you could think of. That was fine with me. I didn't have to stand out on the mound shaking him off all the time.

JIM PRICE, catcher—He didn't catch me often in 1968, but when he did, Jim did a darn good job. I'm not a big stats guy, but Jim caught me in 10 games that year, and my ERA with him behind the plate was 2.28, while opposing batters hit just .189 off me with him catching. As a tandem we must have been doing something right. Plus he hit a walk-off home run as a pinch-hitter off Wilbur Wood of the Chicago White Sox in August. But that's what I mean about everybody on the team. Even the guys who didn't play a whole lot had their moment.

Battery Mates

I worked with a lot of catchers during my career. According to baseball-reference.com, 23 different catchers caught me at some time or other. The list ranges from Bill Freehan, who caught me for 13 years, to Bob Davis, who caught me for only two innings when I was with the San Diego Padres in 1978.

Of course, the catcher I worked with the most—by far—was Freehan. In 1971, for instance, a season in which I threw 376 innings, Bill caught all but 39 of them. He also caught 41 of my 45 starts. In all our years of working together—and I can say this knowing it's absolutely true—we got our signals mixed only three times at most. *Three times!* That's incredible.

It wasn't easy for catchers to catch me, though. That's what I've heard. In other words, that's what they told me. "It's true," Jim Price said. "With Mickey, you really had to be an athletic catcher. You'd set up outside for right-handed hitters because that's where he would try to put his cutter. The outside corner was also an ideal spot for his curveball, but his sinker was the pitch that kept you hopping. You'd set up outside, knowing it could dart in at the feet of a right-handed hitter. So you had to be quick from one side of the plate to the other."

When I first came up to the majors, Gus Triandos would catch me a lot. Gus didn't like it when I didn't throw what he wanted me to throw. He was a guy who'd been around several years, and I was a kid pitcher just up to the big leagues. I was supposed to follow his lead. But no matter what—because this is the way I am—I was going to throw the pitch that was in my head to throw. Being a rookie didn't matter. I was like that my whole career.

After Triandos, Freehan took over, and I didn't have another No. 1 catcher until the Tigers traded me to the New York Mets after the 1975 season. Bill never really got all the attention he deserved. He was such a smart catcher, always thinking along with his pitcher. I was fortunate to have had him behind the plate for all those years.

Price caught me the second most games. But as a runner-up, he was further behind Freehan than I was to Earl Wilson as a long-ball threat. Freehan caught me in 362 games. Price caught me in 40 games total, and Gene Tenace, during my two San Diego Padres years, was a distant third with 27. But a young Tigers catcher who caught me only once has to be mentioned as well because he gave me a unique compliment.

The final game of the 1971 season was memorable for both me and rookie Tim Hosley. Make no mistake, it had already been my best season. With three starts remaining, I'd won 25 games, and everyone was saying that Vida Blue of the Oakland A's and I were the only contenders for the American League Cy Young award. But 25 wins with three starts remaining quickly became 25 with only one start remaining after consecutive 3–2 losses to the Boston Red Sox and New York Yankees. Gone was my chance of winning as many as 28 games. I still had a shot at 26, however. "Vida didn't lead the league in anything," said Reggie Jackson, Blue's longtime teammate, "but his wins were spectacular. Mickey, meanwhile, had one of the great years of all time."

No matter what, it was either going to be me or Blue winning the Cy Young, but finishing on a winning note was pivotal—as was the fact that Blue was the best pitcher on a powerhouse team bound for the playoffs. I went into my last start with a 25–13 record. Blue went into his at 23–8. The Run Support Gods weren't being kind to me, though. In my third to last start, I allowed three runs in the eighth to lose 3–2 in Boston. In my next game, I lost 3–2 again to the Yankees in Detroit. Roy White hit a tie-breaking home run off me to lead off the sixth, while Fritz Peterson shut us down on one hit after the fourth. In my last start, which was also our last game of the season, I lost 2–1 in Cleveland. One of the Indians' runs was unearned because of a rare error at short by Eddie Brinkman.

Hosley, who singled in our only run, was my catcher in that season finale. It was the only time he ever caught me. It was also the last game he caught as a Tiger. He had been with us for two Septembers as a late roster addition. We were only 2–12 in the games he played, but that included a win against the Yankees with him hitting two home runs. He was so giddy after the second one that as he ran the bases he said, "I didn't know where I was. It was really a thrill."

On the last day of the 1970 season, he had caught John Hiller's two-hit 1–0 victory against Cleveland that was played in virtual anonymity. Taking an hour and 41 minutes to complete, the game drew a crowd of only 3,875 at Tiger Stadium. Ike Brown's sacrifice fly in the first inning was the only run we needed.

A year later, in the final game of the 1971 season, I wanted to finish with a win, but I also was pulling for Hosley to take home another game he'd always remember—like Hiller's gem had been for him. In retrospect, we were pulling for each other. But instead of our wishes coming true, we both went home disappointed. Or so I thought. I finished at 25–14, my only three-game losing streak that season. Blue also didn't finish with a flourish, winning just one of his last six starts. Closing out the regular season with an outstanding 1.82 ERA, however, he pitched seven innings of a 7–0 victory against the Milwaukee Brewers.

When it came time to vote for the Cy Young award, American League writers gave Vida 14 first-place votes, I got nine, and Wilbur Wood of the Chicago White Sox received the other one. But here's why I say Hosley didn't go home disappointed that year. Despite the loss he ended up calling the season finale "the most amazing thing" he ever saw. Tim passed away in 2014, but I remember to this day what he said about the game.

As a minor league catcher, he'd never been sure where the pitch being thrown to him would end up. He'd call for one inside or for one outside, but soon learned that didn't mean the ball would be thrown where it was supposed to be thrown. That's minor league baseball for you, though. After that last game in 1971, however, Hosley said the big leagues were entirely different. When he called for a pitch from me on the outside corner, that's where it was thrown. When he called for one inside, that's where it was thrown. He said it was fun after being in the minors "to catch someone who knew what he was doing."

I'm not sure anyone had ever said something so sincerely nice about me—just a pure pitching compliment. But here I'd been hoping he would take home the experience of catching another season-ending gem to match the Hiller finale from the previous season, and he gave me a keepsake instead with his kind comment.

The following year, without breaking it in, Tim made the mistake of wearing a brand new mitt in a spring training game and missed a third strike because of it, costing us a game. The blunder infuriated manager Billy Martin. "I don't like mental mistakes," Martin said. "I can't afford to take a guy north with me who might do something like that."

According to Jim Hawkins, who covered the Tigers for the *Detroit Free Press*, Martin "took mistakes by young players personally because he prided himself on developing them."

Hosley never played in another game for us. After spending the entire 1972 season in Toledo (where he hit 47 home runs in two years) he was traded to Oakland the next spring. But he never forgot he had come up to the majors as a Tiger. And even now I still wish that for him, for me, for both of us—that we would have won that last game.

NORM CASH, first base—God love him, what a personality he was. We all loved Norm. With boyish enthusiasm, he loved playing the game. When you talk about Miguel Cabrera loving to play baseball, Stormin' was the same way.

Our trainer, Jack Homel, mentioned in passing to a group of us that he'd never been on television. Norm picked up on it and while playing in a *Game of the Week* he went over to the tarp near first base to catch a pop-up. He caught the ball, hit the tarp, fell to the ground faking an injury, and never moved. Jack hurried out there, thinking Norm was hurt because he was just lying there flat on his belly. But just as Jack arrived, Norm turned over and said, "See, you're not just on television, you're on *national* television."

Then, of course, there was the time Norm took a table leg up to the plate against Nolan Ryan, saying he could just as easily strike out swinging a table leg as he could a bat. The umpire made him take it back to the dugout and grab a bat. Norm struck out anyway. He also had a trick of putting a game ball in his pocket during infield throws between innings but then handing the scuffed up infield ball to the pitcher while tossing the clean game ball to the dugout. We were able to get away with three or four pitches using a dirty ol' infield ball that did funny things before the batter would ask the ump to check it. Norm was behind the whole thing. I mean, the guy was always doing something out there. He sure made us laugh. We lost him way too early.

DICK MCAULIFFE, second base—The one, the only Mad Dog. He was the guy always trying to get us into a fight. Mac was a very enthusiastic, hard-nosed guy who played the game with pure heart. He was a leadoff batter with a bad habit, though. He'd go up to the plate and even if he struck out he'd come back to the dugout saying, "This guy doesn't have shit today."

On days when we'd get shut out, we had to tell him, "Stop saying that, okay?" The switch from shortstop to second base was a good one for Mac because I remember playing with him in the minors one year, and there'd always be a bunch of empty seats behind first base when the fans found out who was playing shortstop. They didn't trust his arm. As a fierce competitor, though, Mad Dog was a guy you loved having on your side.

RAY OYLER, shortstop—Man, could he play his position. But he couldn't hit a lick. The problem was he got beaned in the minors and never got over it. That's why he was such a bad hitter. Not only did he go 0-for-August in 1968, he nearly went zero-for-the—second half. When we came back from the All-Star break, Ray had a hit in each of his first three games. Everyone was encouraged. But starting on July 14, he went 0-for-36 the rest of the season. Plus he couldn't depend on walks to save his on-base percentage. In his last 32 games that year, he walked once. His OBP during that time was .029.

But Ray always had a sense of humor about the futility with which he swung a bat. After I rode my motorcycle to Tiger Stadium one time, I was out shagging balls in the outfield and all of a sudden I'm looking in at Ray taking batting practice wearing the bike helmet I wore to the ballpark. When I got back to the clubhouse, he came over and said, "I wonder if they'll ever make this legal to hit in. I felt a lot safer wearing it."

One year he did a little bit better at the plate, like he hit over .200, but that was only that one year. He was one of the absolute best I've ever seen at short, though.

DON WERT, third base—Don and I came up to the big leagues the same day. There was nothing fancy about him, but every team needs guys who are consistent above all else. He was very reliable, but it drove him crazy when Freehan would call for my slow, lollipop curveball with big ol' Frank Howard at the plate. We nicknamed Don "Coyote" because Don resembled Wile E. Coyote from the Road Runner cartoons, and when Freehan would call for that curve, Coyote would be standing there at third base with his eyes wide open as if dynamite had just blown up next to him. Don always thought that Howard was going to kill him with a screamer to third on one of those slow curves, but it never happened. Instead of destroying Wert, big Frank would swing at that sucker ball and miss it by three feet. The pitch was never quite where he thought it would be. The highlight of Don's career, of course, was his single that clinched the pennant for us.

WILLIE HORTON, outfielder—What gets overlooked about Willie is how much he studied the game. Thank God he threw out Lou Brock at home plate, but that play was the direct result of Horton doing his homework. First of all, his reaction time while getting to the ball hit to him in left by Julian Javier was excellent because he had positioned himself perfectly and he also knew when he got to the ball that he still had a chance to throw Brock out at home despite Brock's speed. Willie always credits others for helping to make that play—Mickey Stanley for leaping for the ball at short when he had no chance of catching it, Don Wert for making it look like he was going to cut off the throw, and Bill Freehan for making a difficult tag—but Willie was the key player because of how much he had studied Brock's habits on the bases.

I enjoyed having Willie in left. He never embarrassed himself and he hit for power. Plus, you always liked having Willie on your side during a skirmish. He'd been a Golden Gloves fighter in his younger days. The man could take on several players at once, but eventually opponents would just run away from him.

One time we got into a tussle in Kansas City. Two or three guys had grabbed Hank Aguirre and turned him upside down in the stands so that his legs were straight up in the air. We called him Crazy Legs after that. But there were two or three other Kansas City A's players who were mouthing off from the dugout. After seeing what happened to Hank, Willie picked up on what these guys were yelling and took about four steps toward them. He was going to take them all on, but they saw who was coming for them and quickly ran up the steps to the clubhouse. Nobody wanted to mess with Willie.

JIM NORTHRUP, outfielder—Jim was a good ballplayer. He could hit, throw, and run, but he wasn't as good a center fielder as Mickey Stanley. I mean Mickey would give up his life to catch a fly ball—and one time I thought he had done just that. In Chicago he dove onto the warning track to make a catch, and his arms were all bloody from the gravel when he got back to the dugout. But he made that catch against the White Sox.

Center field, however, was the position Northrup always wanted to play. So there was always a conflict about where to use him. Willie Horton was our leftfielder, Al Kaline was in right, so Jim didn't always get the playing time he wanted. I never held it against Northrup for wanting to play every day. I mean, he had a lot of talent, but he just wasn't the outfielder that Mickey was.

MICKEY STANLEY, outfielder—Mickey was an exceptional baseball player, outfielder, and friend. Decades after the World Series, we're still friends. I know Mickey didn't enjoy the 1968

World Series, though. With the shortstop experiment that had him playing out of position, there was just too much pressure on him. But he would sacrifice himself to make a catch. No wonder all the pitchers loved him. Actually, it wasn't just the pitchers. Though he wasn't a superstar, Mickey was the favorite of a lot of Tigers fans.

AL KALINE, outfielder—He was our silent leader, the best player on the team, but not an out-and-out clubhouse leader. That was Norm Cash's job. Al led the team by performing, though. He could hit, he could throw, he could run, he could slide. I mean, he was a perfect ballplayer. When you watched Al, you knew you were watching a Hall of Famer. You can't praise anyone more than that. He was a quiet person, and I know it wasn't easy for him in the majors right away. It wasn't for any of the bonus babies of that generation. The veterans—whose jobs were in jeopardy because the bonus babies existed—didn't want them around, and some of those older players—whose jobs were safe—didn't either. They could be rough on those kids. But Al got over that hump the best way any player could. He proved he could play.

DICK TRACEWSKI, infielder—I really liked Trixie. He was a good utility player who knew what his role was, just a good guy to have on the team. As a side note, though, I loved it when Trixie would talk about how talented Sandy Koufax was as a pitcher. Trixie not only had been a teammate of Sandy's on the Los Angeles Dodgers, but also a roommate, and we loved hearing stories about how good Koufax really was. Plus he was the Dodgers' starting second baseman when Koufax threw his perfect game in 1965. Trixie had a longer career as a coach than he did as a player. In fact, he wore a Tigers uniform in various roles for 28 years—longer than anyone, even Ty Cobb, in the history of the franchise.

GATES BROWN, pinch hitter—When you needed a base hit, you'd get it. When you needed a home run, you'd get it. Gates was one of the best pinch hitters there ever was in baseball. The Gater was a great guy but also a great character. I mean he'd fall asleep in the clubhouse at times while waiting for his one at-bat.

I was sitting right next to him in the dugout the day Mayo Smith called his name to pinch hit when the Gater was eating a hot dog. It was early for him to be pinch-hitting so he was helping himself to a *couple* of hot dogs—not just one. When he heard his name, he just stuffed them inside his shirt. Then he slid headfirst into second while trying to stretch out a single but was called out and had to come back to the dugout with mustard oozing out between his shirt buttons. We were laughing, but Gates wasn't because he knew he'd be fined, which he was, of course. If it had been ketchup, he might have gotten away with it because maybe it would have looked like he had hurt himself. Mustard was a different story. Gater wasn't going to leave those hot dogs behind, though, because he knew they'd be eaten by someone else while he was hitting, so—true story—that's why he stuffed 'em in his uniform.

TOMMY MATCHICK, utility player—A guy who symbolized just how well we got along on that team, Tommy fit right in. He knew he wasn't going to play a whole lot, but he didn't complain, and I imagine most Tigers fans still remember the big home run he hit against the Baltimore Orioles. It was a walk-off home run against Moe Drabowsky on a hot Friday night in July that hit the overhang at Tiger Stadium while a crowd of 53,000 was on hand. The fans went crazy. Tommy's home run gave us a seven-and-a-half game lead over the Cleveland Indians. It might have sounded like a comfortable margin, but we weren't treating it that way. When we stretched the lead to double digits in September, we finally began to breathe a bit easier—but only a bit. Actually, it wasn't until the night of Ernie Harwell's famous "Let's listen to the bedlam" call, which came after Don Wert's single off Lindy McDaniel to drive in Al Kaline with the pennant-clinching run on September 17 that we knew for sure we'd won it.

WAYNE COMER, outfielder—The man who saved my life. Oh yes, he saved my life.

I was the next day's starter, so one day I was out behind the screen near second base during batting practice. That's what the next starter is supposed to do—pick up the batted balls thrown to him and put them in the ball bag. Well, Wayne was out there talking to me. But he wasn't behind the screen. He was off to the side of it. I saw a ball on the grass and when I reached down for it I left myself momentarily unprotected. Just at that point, Willie Horton hit a screamer right at my face. It was the kind of liner that would have done a lot of damage. But luckily Wayne was next to me on the left-field side of the screen. (Guys would stop by all the time to chat, especially outfielders on the way to their positions. It just so happened it was Wayne this time.) Thankfully, he was paying attention to what was going on at the plate like you're taught to do. So when Willie hit the liner, Wayne calmly reached down with his glove and caught the ball just as it was going to smack me in the face. But the force with which his glove was pushed back knocked me flat on my butt. Suddenly, I'm on the ground looking up and wondering, *What the hell was that?*

"Willie's liner was going to hit you, Mick," Wayne said. "I caught it, but the recoil of my glove knocked you down."

"Oh," was all I could say. "Thank you, Wayne."

I had felt the impact of Comer's glove, but if he hadn't been standing there, I hate to think of what might have happened. It was my fault to leave my face exposed as I did. From where I was behind the screen, you're supposed to watch every pitch during batting practice. For a split second, though, I took it for granted that I'd never been hit, nor had I seen anyone else get hit near the screen. I had seen close calls, but this was the closest. So every time I've seen Wayne over the years since or have talked to him on the phone, I say, "How's the man who saved my life?"

He laughs but admits, "Yeah, Mick, you might have been in big trouble if I hadn't been there."

But he *was* there—and so, thank God, was his glove.

151

Pitchers

What did I think of my pitching peers on the Tigers in 1968? I liked almost all of them...many of them a lot. We were friends then. We remained friends after our playing days. Our families also did a lot together. But I had one pretty well-known situation that much was made of because it didn't always go well.

DENNY MCLAIN—When people ask me about Denny, and I get asked about him quite often, I keep it simple. I say he had five years in which he was a damn fine pitcher. And I try to leave it at that. I mean, he won 31 games; then he won 24. He also won two Cy Young awards. He really had some wonderful seasons, but I'm very careful not to say anything about him that's negative because that's how fences never get mended.

What good is it after all these years to rehash whatever differences we had? We were not best friends. People knew that then. They know that now. He was the one who was always ragging on me in the newspapers. Then the reporters would come over to me wondering what he meant. "What do you think, Mickey?" They'd say. "Denny just said this about you."

I know he thought I was jealous of him. Hell, he was a good pitcher. I've always said that. I just don't know why he couldn't keep his mouth shut. I don't know why he did some of the things he did. Why say, "Guys who win 31 games drive Cadillacs; guys who win 17 games ride motorcycles." Why say I was the kind of guy who could piss you off just by saying good morning to you?

And why say he thought that I secretly pulled for us to lose the games I didn't start? Those were hurtful comments.

Denny once wrote that I was miserable in 1968 because he was doing well and I wasn't. He was wrong. I wasn't miserable. I just thought everyone on a team should play by the same rules. But as I say, he was a damn fine pitcher who had some great seasons.

EARL WILSON—He came into his own when the Tigers traded for him in 1966. He'd been a good pitcher for the Boston Red Sox but was even better for us. Heck, when he won 22 games in 1967, Earl was a big reason we almost won the pennant. He was one of the guys that our pitching coach Johnny Sain really helped. Johnny not only was a skilled technician when it came to pitching, but also a mental motivator. A lot of pitchers on a lot of teams responded well to him. I thought the world of him. But he was very selfish about his pitchers. He didn't want any meddling, and managers didn't always like that.

Of course, when you mention Earl to the Tigers fans who remember him, they also remember that he could, and often did, hit for power. In 1968 alone he hit seven home runs for us. In his career, he hit 35 of them. One thing about the home runs Earl hit, though—you pretty much knew right away they were going out of the park. Most of them were no-doubters. He struck out a lot like many pitchers do. But, man, he could hit the ball a mile. He even hit two home runs as a pinch-hitter, including the first home run he ever hit for us—a walk-off shot in 1966 off the Baltimore Orioles' Stu Miller in the 13th inning. That endeared Earl right away to Tigers fans. It also helped that his second home run was a grand slam. And in 1967, also as a pinch-hitter in a six-run ninth at Fenway Park, he connected off future Tigers teammate John Wyatt, who was with Boston then. So when I think back about Earl, I say to myself, "Good hitter, good pitcher…good guy."

JOE SPARMA—I always thought Joe was going to have a better career than he ended up having. But he never achieved the consistency needed to last a long time. I liked Joe. In 1967, bene-fitting from Sain's emphasis on positive thinking, he contributed a lot to our bid for a pennant, but it was pretty much typical Joe. He was inconsistent. For instance, he was 9–1 at the All-Star break but wasn't chosen for the American League team when he should have been. Then he slipped to a 7–8 record after the break. He could look great and then terrible, as every pitcher can. I certainly had my ups and downs.

There were those who thought that not going to winter ball after the 1967 season set him back. Whatever the reason, except for throwing a complete game in our pennant clincher against the New York Yankees—the highlight of his career—his steady progress didn't continue. Plus he had repeated problems with manager Mayo Smith. At one point during the 1968 season, Jeff Samoray for the Society of American Baseball Research wrote that Sparma said, "I don't know that I can pitch for that man anymore."

Joe was vocal. He didn't have much respect for Mayo and sometimes said so. After the 1969 season, the Tigers traded him to the Montreal Expos, where he flopped. In leaving, though, he fired one more insult at Mayo, according to that SABR piece, saying, "He has no idea how to put a pitching staff together. We might have blown two or three pennants in a row."

I always pulled for Joe to keep it together after doing it so impressively during the first half of the '67 season. But he was out of the game before he was 30.

JOHN HILLER—John wasn't the pitcher in 1968 that he would turn out to be later. He had a fastball and an okay curve but didn't add the change-up until after his heart attack in 1971.

We thought he might be done as a player because 27 is awfully young to have a heart attack, but we sure admired how he overcame it to make it back. I know it wasn't easy for him. I've read his comments about desperately needing a job after he recovered and how he could feel the roaches crawling on him as he slept on the floor of the Tigers' minor league clubhouse in Lakeland while helping out as an instructor. I've also read about how he would scrape the mold off the clubhouse food after others were done with it so he could preserve the old bologna for his next meal and how he would save his loose change to afford one beer a week.

It was a challenging time he went through, but more power to him. He not only returned to the big leagues, but he also did so as one of the best relief pitchers in baseball. In 1973 John had

38 saves for us. Joe Coleman won 23 games that year; Hiller saved 11 of them. Jim Perry won 14 games; John saved eight of them. Five of his saves occurred in games I won, so if I didn't thank you then, John—or if I didn't thank you enough—I'm doing so now. I'm glad you made such a great comeback.

PAT DOBSON—Dobber came up through the system and paid his dues in the minors, but you could see he had talent. It was just a matter of when he would make the most of it.

In spurts he made the most of it in 1968, at times looking like one of the best pitchers on the team. He was versatile. Pat could start if asked, but more often he pitched out of the 'pen. It was in June that he won a couple of big games as a starter and had a flurry of four saves. He was another guy who Sain helped. His best years were for other teams, though. He won 20 games one year with the Baltimore Orioles and 19 another year with the New York Yankees. He eventually won more than 120 games in the majors. Oh, and here's something else he did while he was a Tiger. He gave Hiller the nickname "Ratso" because he thought John looked like one of the sleazy characters from the movie *Midnight Cowboy*. It's a nickname Hiller has had for 50 years.

DARYL PATTERSON—When people talk about the big moments of 1968, they have to mention what Daryl did on a July night in Baltimore. In the bottom of the sixth, we were leading the Orioles 2–0 when he came into the game with the bases loaded and no outs. He proceeded to strike out Fred

Valentine, Brooks Robinson, and Davey Johnson to get out of the jam. Years later at a reunion, he called it the biggest game of his career. "I was jacked up big time when I came into that game," Daryl said. "Kaline was playing first base and I remember him saying, 'Go get 'em, D,' when I walked past him. I was probably throwing as hard as I ever threw in my life. You really can do something when you're scared. I think the 3–2 pitch [to Johnson] to end that inning was the best pitch of my career. I was even surprised by it. When it crossed the plate at the knees, I thought, *How the hell did I do that?*"

FRED LASHER—A likable kind of goofy guy who loved to fish. This is what I most recall about Fred: I'm glad I never had to face him as a hitter (except once in 1970) because with that submarine delivery of his, I would have looked ridiculous against him.

He did a nice job for us in 1968, winning five games in relief—all by the same score of 5–4. Fred also had five saves that year, so he was directly involved in 10 of our victories. Nine of those games were while we were putting together a 34–19 record by June 7 as we tried to pull away from the Cleveland Indians. He was a plus for us all year but especially in the first half.

Lasher and Mayo had their differences, but that was mostly after 1968. After being traded to Cleveland in 1970, Fred later said that Mayo didn't know how to handle pitchers. He hoped the Indians would start him against the Tigers so he could prove his point. Fred got a start in 1970, the only one of his career, but it was against the Boston Red Sox, not us. After allowing a run in the first inning and then consecutive home runs to start the second, it was permanently back to the bullpen for him.

JON WARDEN—Jon was one of the funniest guys I've ever met, but we didn't know the humorous side of him when he pitched for us. He was a rookie left-hander out of the bullpen in '68 but quickly made his mark by winning three of our first eight games—two of Denny McLain's starts in relief and one of mine. At one of our reunions, Jon described his early impact this way: "After I won my third game, a guy from *Sports Illustrated* came up to me saying, 'You've pitched three and a third innings so far and you're 3–0. Based on that ratio—a win per inning—what kind of year do you think you're going to have?'

"I replied, 'I should win 45 to 50 games.'"

When Warden was asked years later how he felt about me starting Game 7 of the World Series on two days' rest, he said, "Mayo hadn't sobered up yet from Game 6 so he grabbed his flask and said, 'Go get 'em, Lolo.'"

After getting the win in each of his first three appearances, Jon won only one more game the rest of the year. "My main job was to supply the hot dogs and peanuts," he said.

Then we lost him in the expansion draft to Kansas City, where he hurt his shoulder while with the Royals and never pitched in the majors again. He's become a great ambassador of the game with his humor, but as he's often said, he will never forget being part of the 1968 Tigers because he knows what that championship meant to Detroit. "I've had a lot of people tell me, 'Thanks for saving our city.'"

DON MCMAHON—Don and three others—John Wyatt, Dennis Ribant, and Les Cain—combined for seven victories and four saves in 1968. Their innings pitched ranged from 24 for Cain to McMahon's 35 ⅔. The number of games in which they pitched ranged from Cain's eight (four as a starter) to Wyatt's 22. Individually, they didn't pitch a lot. But taken together, they were 7–3 with a 2.36 ERA in 114 ⅓ innings. In other words, they were extremely useful—and extremely valuable. They were also good guys. I liked them all.

Chapter 14

Game 6

"Oh, is that how you do it?"

—catcher Bill Freehan

Having survived Game 5 at home, we were happy to return to St. Louis. We still faced a hell of a challenge, being down by a game, but you know what? We were taking it step by step.

After all, we were still in this thing. We played good baseball in Game 5. We made the plays we had to make, got the hits we needed to get, and threw the pitches that had to be thrown. If the St. Louis Cardinals weren't taking us seriously yet, all the better. But I believe they were.

Let's face it, though, except for Game 2, everything pretty much had gone their way before we stunned them by coming back in Game 5. But we were way too good a team for the season to end with people laughing at us. *Detroit Free Press* writer Joe Falls wrote that a visiting writer covering the World Series said to him in Detroit that we had been disgracing the

American League. That was tough to read, but I think the entire team felt it wasn't over yet.

The first challenge of the off day before Game 6, however, was for manager Mayo Smith to decide who his starting pitcher would be. But his decision was made easier when Denny McLain announced that his story about having a sore shoulder was false. He'd been setting up a Detroit reporter. And those were Denny's own words. McLain and Mayo weren't initially on the same page, however, when Denny began talking about starting. "I don't know where he got that idea," Mayo told reporters. "I never told him he was the choice."

When Denny was asked about the condition of his shoulder after we got back to St. Louis, he repeated that it had been "a hoax to make a Detroit reporter look bad." At one point on the off day, Falls reported that the confrontation between McLain and reporters trying to find out the truth got so loud and profane that Mayo came out of his office to ask for quiet.

But now Denny was saying his shoulder was fine. That was good news for us, of course. Whoever was going to start Game 6 needed to feel strong—because it would help our hitters to go into the game feeling confident about the guy on the mound. We really hadn't come close to showing what we could do at the plate, but maybe we would against the Cardinals' Ray Washburn.

Meanwhile, Mayo was still saying the starting assignment for Game 6 was between McLain, Earl Wilson, and Joe Sparma. "I don't care what Denny has told anybody," he said. "I can't help what he says. I haven't made up my mind."

Mayo said he would decide in the morning, but the media already were convinced it was going to be Denny. They must have been tipped off. At the same time, McLain, who'd been given a shot of cortisone on the day of Game 5, insisted that "my arm feels as good as it has all year." And that's where the matter stood overnight.

But my impression at the end of the day was that our overall frame of mind was excellent, judging by how relaxed we were during the workout. Even those with a reason to feel pressure didn't sound like they did. For instance, in batting practice, hitless Bill Freehan (0-for-16) was watching Jim Northrup knock line drives to the outfield that would have been hits during a game. But instead of sounding frustrated, Bill merely said, "Oh, is that how you do it?"

The biggest motivation was that we knew everything would be equal if we could just win Game 6. We'd no longer be in a hole.

Mayo confirmed the next morning that Denny was his choice, and it quickly looked like a good one. *The Detroit News* columnist Jerry Green wrote in his book, *Year of the Tiger*, that "in the first inning, it was apparent McLain was sharp again. He fired the baseball, placing it where he wanted."

With our bats springing to life, it wasn't long before we were in complete command. A 10-run third inning did the trick. But in reality, the two runs we scored in the second off Washburn would have been enough. What was good for us all to see, however, was that Freehan drove in the second run with a single to left, his first hit of the World Series. The monkey was off his back.

What was even better were those 10 runs we scored in the third inning on the way to a 13–1 rout. I mean, what an inning. Northrup hit a grand slam, Al Kaline and Norm Cash had two hits each in the same inning, and by the time the dust settled—which it eventually did—we had sent 15 batters to the plate.

The Cardinals had beat us up 10-1 in a soggy Game 4 in Detroit. We returned the favor in Game 6, which also encountered some rain, by the way. But by the time the game was delayed for 49 minutes in the eighth inning, the ballpark was nearly empty. With the Cardinals behind by a bunch, maybe 5,000 fans were still in their seats.

As for McLain, the story wasn't so much how he pitched but how we hit. His run support allowed him to be aggressive the entire way. "I just threw strikes," he said. "I challenged hitters all afternoon. It's not hard with a 13-run lead."

The Cardinals scored their only run on Julian Javier's two-out single in the bottom of the ninth. All nine of their hits were singles, in fact. We had nine hits, too, but not all singles. Our attack featured a run-scoring double from Willie Horton in the second, a solo home run from Kaline off Steve Carlton in the fifth, and Northrup's grand slam off Larry Jaster in the third. Then again, our third inning was something to behold—a parade of runs. Hits, walks, they just kept coming.

By the time McLain, the ninth batter of the inning, bunted his way into being the first out, there'd been three walks, three singles, a pitch that hit Don Wert, and Northrup's grand slam.

"All I wanted to do was to hit a sacrifice fly," Northrup said. "When I try to hit home runs, I don't do it."

Northup was no stranger to slams, of course. He once was referred to as a grand slam specialist, and I can see why that was the case. The grand slam he hit in Game 6 was his fifth of the season, the eighth of his career. Two of his slams earlier in the season came in successive innings against the Cleveland Indians.

But suddenly the World Series didn't just appear to be even, it *was* even. The Cardinals had won Games 3 and 4 by combined scores of 17–4. We took Games 5 and 6 by combined scores of 18–4. Bob Gibson had won two games for St. Louis. I had won two games for us. Now we would face each other again. "I'd rather not have to pitch," Gibson told reporters, "but it really makes no difference. I'll be ready." His words offered us some hope, however. "I got tired in the sixth or seventh inning the other day," Gibson said, referring to Game 4, "and maybe I'll tire earlier this time. But, as I said, I'll be ready."

Fatigue, in other words, was going to be a factor. If I could keep us close until Gibson tired, if indeed he was going to, we'd have a chance—maybe even a good chance—of winning.

But I was going to be starting on two days' rest, and Gibson would be starting on three. On paper, that appeared to be a disadvantage for us. As they say, though, the game isn't played on paper.

This might surprise you, but I was pleased Game 7 was going to be played in St. Louis. Nothing against Tiger Stadium, but being a relative bandbox, it was difficult to pitch there anytime. Working on two days' rest probably would have made the ballpark feel even smaller.

"The bigger park might forgive a pitching mistake," I said at the time. "Fatigue gives you a better chance of making that mistake. I'll be able to throw all right. I'll have a good fastball, but I probably won't have my good, snapping curve."

As usual, I thought Lou Brock would present a unique challenge. I had tried everything else, so I told reporters before the game that I might pitch underhand to him.

I didn't. But it was worth a thought.

Chapter 15

Highs and Lows

"That sucker came off the table. It was fantastic."
—pitching coach Johnny Sain

We were blessed to have Johnny Sain, a great pitching coach, working with us in 1968.

He'd been an excellent pitcher in his day, a 20-game winner four times. Another claim to fame was the Boston Braves' slogan that called for "Spahn and Sain and pray for rain." The phrase was coined when the National League race in 1948 came down to the last two weeks of September. As the core of Boston's rotation, Warren Spahn and Sain helped the Braves win their first pennant in 34 years.

Spahn was a star, of course. He's deservedly in the Hall of Fame. But Sain was exceptional as well, a pitcher in tune with his talents as a player and then as a coach. My career, I freely admit, would not have been what it was without the coaches who shaped it. To begin with, I didn't know what I was doing when I became a professional pitcher. With me at 21 threatening to retire back in Portland, Gerry Staley saved my career by teaching me how to throw strikes. I had my next job all picked out. I would have been a mailman if Staley, a four-time major league All-Star, hadn't transformed me from thrower to pitcher. But Sain was just as pivotal in my development because he made me a more positive person. In turn, that helped to fine-tune me as a pitcher.

Johnny came to the Tigers in 1967 with a reputation for not just being a pitching coach but a pitchers' coach. There's a difference. One involves a skill; the other is about individuals. It was a well-deserved reputation. We loved the guy. I know he quickly helped Earl Wilson as a pitcher. In Sain's first year with Detroit, Earl became a 22-game winner. He also had a positive influence on Denny McLain.

However, Sain ran the pitching staff more than Mayo Smith, the manager, did. That was the case wherever Sain coached. He didn't want the team's manager interfering with his starting rotation or his bullpen. Actually, he didn't want the manager around his pitchers at all. Some managers didn't mind his proprietary approach, but there were those who did, which is probably why Sain coached for so many teams. He insisted on running things his way.

Where Sain excelled was in his concentration on the mental side of the game. He was a psychologist as well as an instructor, a mentor as well as a technician. He understood pitchers as people, as if they all had unique personalities, which he believed they did.

I'm not saying he was deficient on the teaching side. He knew pitching. It's just that he excelled at getting into your head.

With every pitcher on his staff, he wanted to know what his interests were, what his hobbies were. When he learned what they were, he'd go to a library or a bookstore to find out as much about them as he could. He felt he could better relate to his pitchers that way. If you were into history, he would talk history with you. I was into motorcycles, so he learned about motorcycles. Denny was into airplanes, so Sain talked to him about flying. Plus, he'd been a pilot himself. In fact, he was such a good pilot that they kept him stateside during World War II as a flight instructor.

With pilots and pitchers, he must have had the same effect.

Sain would wander around the outfield during batting practice. He'd watch whoever was throwing on the side that day, of course, but he made sure to touch base with each of his pitchers—either talking about their interests or maybe just asking how things were going. With his relief pitchers, Sain would try to find out if they were mentally prepared to pitch that night. That could be based on matters such as who was having a problem at home and who wasn't. Meanwhile, it gave him an idea about who to use in any given game—and who to stay away from.

The philosophy he took with him wherever he went was that he believed that the manager should control the position players and that he, as the pitching coach, should be totally in charge of the pitching staff. Though it sometimes got him in trouble, Sain also felt a manager should turn to him to decide who to warm up because only he would know who was the most mentally ready to pitch. It was always about the readiness to pitch in the now—not who threw well yesterday or two days before. Part of that theory, though, was Sain's focus on one's mental state. As it said in his 2006 obituary in *The New York Times*, "he lugged around books and tapes advocating the virtues of positive thinking."

The best way to describe the experience of pitching for Sain is that I once pitched a game against the Baltimore Orioles in which I got knocked out in the second inning. I was fuming, but the next thing I knew, Sain was sitting on a stool alongside me. "I want to talk to you about the game," he said.

"I don't want to talk about the damn game, Johnny," I answered back. "You saw it. I got shelled."

That wasn't his point. "No, no, no," he said. "You threw a curveball to Brooks Robinson that was one of the best curveballs I've ever seen you throw."

I believe I replied by saying, "Well, so what?"

"Do you remember how you held it?" he said. "That sucker came off the table. It was fantastic."

Two days later, I was down in the bullpen throwing to Hal Naragon, who caught in the big leagues but later followed Sain wherever he went as his bullpen coach. Naragon told me to start throwing some breaking balls. So I started spinning them up there. "Mick, that's not the one you threw to Brooks," Naragon said. "Throw me the one you threw to Brooks."

He obviously had spoken with Johnny. As a tag team, they were still trying to find my curveball. I tried to throw one, but it just wasn't there. I threw a few more, and then all of a sudden, Naragon jumped up, saying, "That's the one, Mick, that's the one!"

Sain was standing nearby. "Throw another," he said.

I threw another, then another. All three were great curveballs. "Put that one in your back pocket," he told me. "Next time you're out there, that's the one to throw. Now you're done for the day."

Done for the day when I'd just found it? Sain wouldn't let me throw another pitch, and here's why: his mission had been accomplished. I couldn't wait to throw the curve again that I'd just thrown. That's how Sain operated. Every time a guy did something wrong, such as when I lasted only two innings, he wouldn't even mention it. He would directly go to what you did well.

He'd get it in your head so firmly, in fact, that you couldn't wait to go back out there and pitch with a positive attitude. That's why all the pitchers loved him.

By 1969, however, Johnny had clashed with Mayo about how to best condition pitchers. And his stint with the Tigers was over. Too bad. We missed him when he was gone. He'd been a great motivator.

Taking On "the Express"

I had a couple of epic duels in my career against Nolan Ryan, winning one, losing the other. They both lasted into extra innings. It wasn't uncommon for me to pitch beyond the ninth, especially during the 1970s when I was taking on my heaviest workload. Speaking of that, one of the things I'm most proud of is that I pitched an average of 330 innings from 1971 to 1974.

I've always thought that '71 was my best individual season. I won 25 games that year. But my ERA was lower in 1972 (2.50) than it was in 1971 (2.92). Keep in mind that durability defined me as a pitcher every bit as much as the three games I won in the World Series. For instance, I threw 195 complete games. Through 1972, I was 112–15 in them. From 1973 on, during our decline as a team, I was 39–29. But some of my most memorable games—both good and bad—occurred during the same decline. I pitched into extra innings 13 times in my career. Five times I won, five times I lost, and the three other games lasted beyond the point at which I exited.

A clash in 1974 against Ryan might have been the best regular-season game of my career. Don't get me wrong. I was outpitched in the game. I struck out four; Ryan struck out 19.

I allowed 10 hits; Ryan allowed four. But we won the game 1–0 in 11 innings. John Wockenfuss didn't have to face Ryan that night, but I remember what he told reporters after the game about Nolan's vaunted fastball. "He grunts when he throws it,"

Wockenfuss said, "but by the time you hear the grunt, the ball is in the catcher's glove behind you."

We weren't going anywhere as a team that season, and the game was played at night in Anaheim, so it didn't get as much immediate attention. But the following day, because of the remarkable showdown it turned out to be—with Ryan striking out 19 for the second time in three starts—it got the play it deserved back in Detroit and elsewhere. "I'd seen Nolan for the first time in 1966, down in A ball," said Gene Lamont, our catcher in the 1–0 game. "I remember thinking to myself, *This is going to be rough if they're all like this in pro ball*. But Mickey did a good job of keeping the ball down. Yeah, I remember that game. It was a classic."

It was definitely a classic but so was the first of our extra-inning duels that Nolan won in 1973 at Tiger Stadium. I was not the losing pitcher in that game. Lerrin LaGrow was. But it was an endurance test all the same, one in which I lasted 11 innings, while Ryan was able to last all 12. He didn't have his best control that day, walking eight, but we were just 2-for-17 against him with runners in scoring position, so it was a frustrating game for us from beginning to end. But even struggling with his control, Ryan was impressive. The game finally ended on his 205th pitch. I pitched okay in that 1973 game. I allowed 10 hits but didn't walk anyone, which helps to explain how the California Angels had only four at-bats with a runner in scoring position. But with the score tied at three since the sixth inning, I still didn't last as long as Ryan did.

Unfortunately, the Angels jumped on LaGrow right away for two runs in the top of the 12th, and you darn well knew that Ryan was not about to hand the game over to someone else once he had the lead. With his high pitch count, he had to be tired, but down to our final at-bats, we didn't even get the ball out of the infield against him as he closed out the game.

Now we were facing him again on August 20, 1974, in Anaheim, and Ryan's fastball was at its absolute best. "He was the fastest I'd ever seen him," said our manager Ralph Houk.

I got a kick out of how one of our outfielders, Dick Sharon, described Ryan to Jim Hawkins of the *Detroit Free Press*. "I thought he was *The Exorcist*. He scared the devil out of me."

I knew what I was up against and said so. "Sure, it makes a difference to pitch against him," I said about the matchup with Ryan. "I don't get pumped up to the extent that I get all excited, but I did start concentrating early on what I was going to do. I had a gameplan ready. You knew it was going to be tough."

With Ryan becoming the first pitcher ever to strike out 19 twice in his career, it was going to be tougher than tough. But fortunately there was a significant difference in how the two teams ran the bases. Lamont threw out the two Angels who attempted to steal against us. Speedy Mickey Rivers, who got caught in a rundown between second and third with one out in the bottom of the ninth, was the second of the two. However, we were successful on two of our first three attempts, which gave Houk the confidence to give Ben Oglivie the steal sign with two outs in the top of the 11ᵗʰ—despite the suspicion that Ryan would pitch out to keep him from stealing. "I had to gamble," Houk said. "What the hell, we weren't hitting the ball anyway." To our surprise, Ryan did not pitch out, and Oglivie slid into second safely. Bill Freehan followed with a single for the only RBI he ever had in 38 plate appearances against Ryan. "As I remember, it was a jam shot to right," Lamont said, "but it got the run in. I remember how dominating Ryan was that day. My hitting highlight was that I struck out only once."

When we scored that run, I became extra determined to finish what I had begun, so I went back out for the bottom of the 11ᵗʰ. I don't even know what my pitch count was, but it wasn't low. "I'd say at least 150," Lamont said.

I gave up a leadoff single to start the Angels' 11ᵗʰ, and, sure enough, they bunted the runner to second. But Bobby Valentine grounded out to third for the second out, and after a really smart intentional walk to Frank Robinson, Bob Oliver flied out to right to end the game.

What a great game it had been. I wish it had meant more than giving us a 58–65 record at the time, but decades later I still think of what took place that night and I smile.

There are other games of which I'm not so fond. After all, I gave up four walk-off home runs in my career. In 1972 against the New York Yankees, I also allowed a ninth-inning home run—an upper-deck shot—to relief pitcher Lindy McDaniel with the score tied. We came back to tie that late September game in the bottom of the ninth, but I allowed another solo shot to Roy White in the 12th inning to lose it. With only six games left and with us in the middle of a pennant race, it looked like a defeat that could cost us a playoff spot. But because we won our next five games, it didn't.

I made up for those home runs by McDaniel and White by bouncing back four days later with a 4–1 complete-game victory against Boston, a game in which I struck out 15, one short of my career high. That victory against the Red Sox put us back in first place. Two days later we won the American League East. But we lost the American League Championship Series to the Oakland A's.

There's one more extra-inning outcome I don't like discussing because it was my fault that we lost it. In the first week of the 1973 season, I took a scoreless game into the 10th inning against the Baltimore Orioles before losing 1–0 on an unearned run. I know for sure it was unearned because I made the bad throw to third base that allowed the deciding run to score.

Then again, I had always liked my chances of winning when I went the distance—and I always felt it was my job to pitch the entire game. I was a starting pitcher for 14 years in the big leagues and in the first 10 I averaged 11 complete-game victories per season. I'm proud of that—way prouder than of the darn home run I gave up to McDaniel and of my stupid throw to third—that's for sure.

Hot-N-Ready

I've known two owners of the Tigers—John Fetzer, for whom I played, and Mike Ilitch, for whom I once worked. Ilitch and I weren't close. But there was a time I thought we were going to be.

In 1968 we didn't know each other at all. But when the Tigers became the talk of the town—and especially when it looked like we were going to win the American League pennant and maybe more—it didn't take long to hear from him. Little Caesars pizza was in its infancy back then, getting off the ground as it began to build its Hot-N-Ready empire. It wasn't until more than 20 years later that Ilitch bought the Tigers, but on our way to winning it all, I found out how big a fan he was.

Mike was as excited as anyone about our success. That's because he had been a player in the Tigers' organization. He knew his baseball. He definitely did and he was a Detroiter through and through. So, of course, he was thrilled when we won. The whole city was. But he also knew—as did his wife Marian—that it would be good for business to be closely associated with a winning team and to have a Tigers player as a company spokesman. So about a month before the World Series, Little Caesars contacted me about signing autographs at stores that would soon open in nearby Flint and Utica, Michigan. I agreed to sign, but the season was still going on, so we let it go until later. There was a lot of baseball still to play before I could make those appearances.

I did not forget what I had agreed to do, however. Well, the World Series ended on a Thursday, and I was supposed to make those two appearances on a Saturday two days later. But as soon as we won, I heard there was a big discussion at Little Caesars about whether I would honor my commitment. Ilitch was part of those discussions, and I heard he stood up at the meeting to say, "Look, I don't know Mickey personally, but he seems to be a trustworthy guy. So I'll bet everyone at this meeting $1,000 he'll be ready to go when the time comes."

I guess the response to that was, "C'mon, Mike, Mickey won't be there. He might not even be in town. He'll probably be elsewhere celebrating."

Without even knowing me, Ilitch had defended me. That really impressed me when I heard it. "No, he'll be there," he had said on my behalf. "He's going to live up to the agreement."

To be certain I would, however, Ilitch drove over to my house on that Saturday morning, came right up to the front door, knocked, and said, "Hello, I'm Mike Ilitch from Little Caesars."

I replied, "Okay, let me get my coat" and got in the car. He drove me up to Flint, where we were mobbed by tons of fans. But because of how big the crowd was, we were late leaving for Utica. Two things happened on our way there.

As he drove, we talked, and as we talked, we reached a business agreement. Ilitch hired me to represent Little Caesars at all his new store openings. But because I could write my own ticket on a lot of stuff at that point as the World Series MVP, I told him I wanted to be more than just a front man. I wanted to learn the pizza business from the bottom up, so that I could be part of Little Caesars after I got out of baseball. "I have every intention of doing that with you, Mickey," Ilitch told me. With that, I agreed to a two-year contract right then and there in the car.

Everything went well between us initially, but at the end of the second year right around the Christmas holidays, I got a letter saying my services were no longer needed at Little Caesars. "What the hell did I do wrong?" I wanted to know.

I hadn't done anything wrong, I soon learned. My lawyer, Bob Fenton, called Ilitch asking why the hell he let me go. We both thought I had done a great job for the company. It turned out that Ilitch thought so, too. But he was a shrewd business-man even then, and, frankly, it didn't matter what kind of job I had done for him. "Look, every time Mickey pitches a game, people think of Little Caesars," Ilitch told us. "Every time he's on TV, they think of Little Caesars. Wherever Mickey goes, they think of Little Caesars. Why should I pay him when I've got him for free?"

It was a business decision pure and simple—a matter of brand recognition and cost efficiency. Nothing more, nothing less.

What also happened two days after the World Series as we drove from Flint to Utica was that we got pulled over for speeding. Ilitch was the one driving, trying to make up for the time we lost in Flint. A state trooper came up to the car to ask where we were going in such a hurry, and Mike replied with urgency in his voice: "I have to get this guy to Utica! He's supposed to be signing autographs at Little Caesars! We're way behind schedule!"

"Who is this guy?" The officer asked, not knowing who else was in the car.

"It's [bleeping] Mickey Lolich sitting here!" Ilitch replied. "He's fresh off winning three games against the St. Louis Cardinals."

"Well, I'll be damned," the trooper said. "You better get going or else you'll be late."

So off to Utica we rapidly went. Mike was at the wheel with his foot still firmly planted on the pedal. We got there late but not too late. I don't think any of the fans waiting for us had left early. The crowd, as you might expect, was huge again. We had fun that day. I thought we'd be associates for many years. But it was two and out.

I never again heard from Ilitch after Little Caesars let me go. My hopes of learning the pizza business abruptly ended, which disappointed me. When he owned a professional softball team, we were walking toward each other at a game one time, but I avoided him. It wasn't until Comerica Park opened in 2000 that we met again. I got on an elevator that he and his wife were already on. I didn't see him right away, but suddenly I heard someone ask, "Can you still pitch?"

Recognizing the voice, I looked around and saw him. "The curveball isn't what it used to be," I replied. Then I reached over to shake his hand. I also gave Marian a hug. That's the first time I had spoken to Ilitch since he had let me go more than

30 years before and I never saw him again after that. But I also never forgot what he had said about me: "Why should I pay him when I've got him for free?"

That was his reasoning for firing me. It hurt at the time, but I couldn't argue with the logic. And even if I could argue with it, there was nothing I could do about it. The man had made up his mind.

Chapter 16

Game 7

"Now I'll finish it for you."

—Mickey Lolich

Bear with me. I need to say this first. Why talk about a great World Series—like this one—and leave the outcome until the end, as if you still don't know what the hell happened? So you probably can guess what I'm going to say next because it's not like it took place yesterday.

We *won* the 1968 World Series, and after all these years, it still feels great to say that the Tigers were the champions of baseball.

We'd been underdogs the entire postseason. But remember the entire postseason consisted of only the World Series because additional levels of the playoffs did not exist back then. There were no division series, no championship series. But winning the American League pennant was every bit as big as it is now. It was big enough, for instance, for us to dunk our dignified owner John Fetzer in the whirlpool tank when we won it. Take

183

it from one of those who helped pick him up and dunk him. I'll never forget the look on his face and what Mr. Fetzer said when he popped up from the water. "Now I feel part of this celebration, boys," he said with the widest grin I ever saw on his face.

The stairway to a championship in 1968 had only two steps: you won the pennant and then you went to the World Series. It was a simpler time for baseball. Nobody had given us much of a chance against the defending champion St. Louis Cardinals, and fewer still could see us winning after we lost three of the first four games. But we ended up as champions all the same.

And our tough, blue-collar city—still reeling from the riots the year before—went wild with joy. What an exciting journey it was. Probably every team says that when it wins, and they all mean it. We meant it, too. Right to the final pitch of the final inning, it wasn't easy. But before we travel through the seventh game together, let me answer your first question even before you ask it: was I nervous to be starting Game 7 with such stars as Bob Gibson and Lou Brock on the other side? I was not. My wife insists I slept like a baby the night before.

Catapulting us into a winner-take-all finale were victories in our previous two games. We played good baseball in Game 5 to save ourselves with a 5–3 victory at Tiger Stadium. Then after traveling to St. Louis—down a game but loose and confident—we clobbered the Cardinals 13–1 in Game 6. As knowledgeable baseball people have said many times for many years, however, momentum is only as good as your next day's starting pitcher, so both Gibson and I were acutely aware of how much the outcome of the World Series depended on us.

Having won two games each, we were well matched but not well rested. Gibson was starting on three days' rest. I was starting on only two. As far as facing the same challenge, though, all was equal. The spoils would likely go to whichever of us was about to pitch better.

My family, of course, was hugely excited about Game 7. After thinking they'd watch it on television, my dad and Uncle Frank were so determined not to miss it that they bought a couple of one-way plane tickets from Detroit to St. Louis. But because return flights were all booked, they weren't sure when they could get back. Neither of them seemed to be nervous on my behalf, though. "Mickey has always had ice in his veins when the chips are down," my mother said about me.

My biggest problem the morning of Game 7 was finding enough time to eat my breakfast before it got cold. Between waiting at the hotel in St. Louis for the tickets I ordered, trying to help family members get organized, and the team's traveling secretary saying it was already time to get on the bus to the ballpark, I ordered an omelet three times, and three times it got cold.

I took about three bites before boarding the bus hungry. But my mind still was more on the logistics of others—like finding a return flight to Detroit for my father and uncle—than it was on the upcoming game. I know that should not have been the case, but it was. Luckily, during batting practice, I saw Tigers general manager Jim Campbell sitting in his seat, looking at the field. "Hey, Jim," I said to him. "I want to make a deal with you."

"What kind of deal?" He growled back at me. That's the kind of guy Campbell was—at least on the outside. Gruff.

"My dad and uncle have flown here from Detroit," I told him, "but to fly home, they couldn't get tickets for another two days. I'll tell you what: if I win this game for you, let them fly home on the team airplane after the game. Okay?"

"Consider it done," Campbell replied. "They'll fly home with us."

Easier said than done? Maybe.

"Fine," I said, and walked away. But I knew where to find Campbell if I needed to later because he never once left his seat.

About the second inning, I walked off the mound with the game scoreless, and there was Campbell in his seat looking at me. I gave him the thumbs-up sign. He did not respond. About the third or fourth inning, same thing, no score, and I gave him another thumbs-up. Still no response. That's because he was nervous about the outcome. I didn't blame him. He did not want to jinx us by responding to my displays of confidence.

But as much as I still could, I was treating Game 7 as just another ballgame. I mean that. I approached it with this thought: I wasn't facing Gibson. I was facing the other eight guys in the lineup. My job was to get them out, just like any other time. It wasn't like any other time, of course, and with all eyes squarely on the starting pitchers, it helped that the game began well. But it began well for both starters.

We went into the game with what some thought of as offensive momentum, having outscored the Cardinals 18–4 in the previous two games. But with a pitcher like Gibson on the mound for the opposing team, we knew that didn't mean much. The game could be decided by one timely hit or one untimely blunder, and those weren't matters of momentum. But there was momentum in our attitude. We wanted to win for ourselves, naturally. But we also wanted to win for the fans, the city, and each other.

So when we scored three runs in the seventh, I walked up to manager Mayo Smith and tapped him on the shoulder. He had originally said he expected only five innings from me that day. He asked after the fifth if I could pitch one more. After the sixth inning, he asked again. Both times I said I could keep going. But when I tapped him on the shoulder going into the bottom of the seventh, it wasn't about pitching just one more inning. "I'll finish this thing for you now," I told him.

"That's exactly what I wanted to hear," he replied.

As I walked out of the dugout in the bottom of the seventh to head for the mound, I gave Campbell a thumbs-up for the third time, but this time he gave it right back to me. And, sure enough, when I got on the team bus heading to the airport, my dad and uncle were on it, too. More than that, as the father of the winning pitcher, everyone was congratulating my dad. He was like a hero.

Back in the first inning, though, we didn't yet know how it was going to turn out. Gibson looked like Gibson as he retired the side in order. The spotlight wasn't new to him. He had started and won the seventh game of both the 1964 and 1967 World Series. I wasn't as efficient initially. A couple of Cardinals got on base in the first inning, including a single and stolen base by Curt Flood before Mike Shannon flied out to center for the third out.

But here's what I want to tell you. I went into the seventh game with the feeling of immunity. I was being asked to pitch on two days' rest. I'd already done well in Game 2, had done well in Game 5, and if I wasn't successful in Game 7, nobody was going to hold it against me, especially the great fans of Detroit. They'd say, "Damn, Mickey, you went out and you tried." With that in my mind, I took the mound relaxed. I had no problems whatsoever. People were amazed how relaxed I was. But that's how I was from the moment I woke up that day.

For instance, I did a daily radio show during the World Series. We'd talk at 7:00 AM Detroit time, which was 6:00 AM in St. Louis. But on the morning of the seventh game, the people at the station were wondering if they should call me because of how much was at stake. They didn't want to piss me off. They didn't want to mess with my process of getting ready.

Well, they ended up calling, but the host, Dick Purtan, said right away that he didn't want to bother me. I was free to go back to sleep if I needed to. "No bother, Dick," I said. "What are your questions?"

"How do you feel about starting Game 7 on short rest?" He asked.

"I can rest all winter," I replied.

I answered a few more questions, and then when he hung up, I went back to sleep. I guess that's called being relaxed.

Brock, of course, was the first hitter I faced. I pitched him a different way in this game. I tried going inside against him instead of outside. In his first at-bat against me in Game 5, he had doubled to left. This time he grounded out to second, so I must have gotten the pitch inside enough. Whether I did or didn't, it felt good to keep Lou off base after all the trouble he had caused. He was 4-for-8 against me in my other two starts and 8-for-17 overall in the first six games. Anytime he made an out, it was to be savored. *Finally* is what I said to myself after his first at-bat.

At some point after the first inning, even while the Cardinals were still scoreless, Bill Freehan came out to the mound asking me, "What's bothering you, Mickey?" He said he noticed a strange look on my face. It wasn't pitching related, but he was right. Something was bothering me. "I didn't get any breakfast, and I'm hungrier than hell," I told him.

All those omelets that had gotten cold and hadn't been eaten before the bus left were coming back to haunt me. Three bites had been my entire breakfast. I also hadn't eaten anything in the clubhouse. So here we were—a catcher and pitcher conversing at the mound in the seventh game of the World Series with millions of viewers probably wondering what we were talking about. My fastball? My breaking ball? No, our discussion was about my empty stomach. "I'll get a burger for you between innings," Bill told me there at the mound. He didn't personally go get one for me. I mean, he didn't run out in his uniform to the concession stand, but he did ask one of the clubhouse kids to do it—only to be told, "That would be a little tough right now."

I think they were getting the clubhouse ready for a possible celebration. I mean, someone was going to win this thing, and we had as good a chance as they did. But, darn, no burger. However, they brought a couple of candy bars to the dugout in case I wanted them. Meanwhile, I continued to pitch with my stomach rumbling. I was also pitching tired, but that had its advantages. Pitches move more when you're tired and maybe not throwing with as much velocity as you usually do. Therefore, my sinker was really moving that day.

I was also feeling a little weak, which meant to a friend of mine that we were going to win the game. Seriously, I had a friend who always wanted to know how I felt whenever I pitched. I think it was his way of figuring out how we'd do that day. Every time I would tell him I didn't feel 100 percent, he'd say I was going to win because he knew the history of how my pitches moved when I was "a little weak."

When I walked Tim McCarver to start the bottom of the second, I imagine there were those already getting worried about Game 7. At that point three of the six batters I had faced had gotten on base. Manager Mayo Smith was one of those already nervous because, as broadcasters like to say, there was "some stirring" in our bullpen after McCarver got on.

I admit I wasn't putting the ball where I wanted. My curve was missing but not to the point that I thought I was struggling. Even so, I needed to start throwing more strikes, a process that fortunately began with the next batter. With McCarver on first, Roger Maris—playing the last game of his career—hit a one-hopper to Mickey Stanley at short for the start of a double play. Equally important, as far as I was concerned, was that I'd thrown a good pitch to Maris on a 1–2 count—the first sign I had begun to locate my pitches better. Several more good signs followed—to the extent that it wasn't until I had retired eight in a row that the Cardinals had another base runner.

Stanley (the outfielder who was moved to shortstop for the series) made a fine play on the ball Maris hit to him in the second, by the way. When I watched the replay years later, I got a kick out of Harry Caray saying to Curt Gowdy on TV, "Are you sure he's never played shortstop?"

The other thing I noticed on the replay was, uh, what a big potbelly I had. The problem for us, though, wasn't how I was pitching as much as how well Gibson was pitching. We didn't have a runner until Stanley's infield single with one out in the fourth. Not only that, but six of our first 12 outs were on strikeouts, including four on called strikes. We'd known from the outset that we would be in trouble if Gibson was at his best, and so far it looked like he was. But we had this shred of hope: it wasn't until after the fifth inning that Gibson had begun to tire in Game 4, so maybe he would eventually feel some fatigue at the same point in Game 7. We could only hope.

I wasn't matching Gibson strikeout for strikeout, nor was I trying to, but I was throwing a lot of sinking fastballs—so many, in fact, that in the third and fourth, the Cardinals hit into five ground-outs. As long as I was getting quick outs on the ground, it didn't matter if I was striking anyone out. This is what I told reporters later: "I began to get the feeling out there that they had tighter sphincters than we did."

But at the same time, as I went into the bottom of the fifth inning of a scoreless game, I didn't know how much longer

I would last. As I said, Mayo initially wanted five innings from me, but I would never say no if he wanted more. At the moment I just wanted to get through the fifth, especially after McCarver's leadoff single—a hit that didn't mean I was tiring, however. As Caray said on the broadcast, I "was showing no signs at all of deteriorating."

As it turned out, McCarver didn't get anywhere in the fifth because I struck out Maris and got the next two hitters, Dal Maxvill and Gibson, on pop-ups. Still scoreless, it wasn't until the bottom of the sixth that the events that would start shaping the outcome of Game 7 began to take place.

The first of those followed Brock's leadoff single.

I'd gotten Lou out in his first two at-bats with grounders to second, but this time I threw him a pitch too far outside, and he sprayed it to left, as he loved doing the entire series.

What Brock would try to do next was no secret. He had his sights set on second base. And if the point at which we were in the game didn't make that obvious, the size of Brock's lead from first base did. If nothing else, he was daring me to throw over to first so he could take off for second.

With one wave of his bare hand, Norm Cash tipped me off that Brock would be running on the next throw to first. We had something set up so that when Norm felt Lou was going, he would take a step or two toward me. He'd be faster on his throw to second base that way. It also helped that Brock slid right into Stanley's tag at second for the out instead of to the outside of the bag. Even so, it was very close and might have been challenged had replay been part of the game back then.

I'm not saying Brock would have been called safe, but it was close. That play not only demonstrates how many little things we did right, but also how many we needed to do right to keep Brock off the bases. Cash's throw to second was perfect, but you have to credit Stanley for a quick tag as well. Brock would have been safe if Stanley hadn't gotten his glove down as fast as he did.

Erasing Brock as a base runner was important, but he wasn't the only Cardinal who could steal second. And with two outs in the sixth, their other speedster, Flood, who'd stolen three bases in six games, got on base with an infield single. But Flood's lead from first base was nowhere near as big as Brock's had been—about two strides shorter, in fact—so when he took off for second as I threw over to first, he didn't get far before he was caught in a rundown, which we executed flawlessly except for me. I held onto the ball too long, nearly colliding with Flood. I don't know how many steps I took, running him back to second, but I took too many. Fortunately it didn't cost us.

Players weren't as demonstrative back then as they are now, but what a big inning that was for us, picking off both Brock and Flood to keep the game scoreless, as it went to the seventh. For all I knew at the time, though, I was done for the day.

The seventh inning didn't look different at first from any previous inning. When Stanley took a called third strike followed by Al Kaline's grounder to third, it could safely be said that we weren't yet getting to Gibson. But with two outs and the bases empty, Cash singled to right on a full count. A difference in baseball eras helped him, though. During that at-bat Cash checked his swing on a 1–1 pitch, which might have been called a strike on an appeal today. But appeals to base-line umpires were rare in 1968—if indeed they existed at all. The home-plate umpire almost always had the last word. Therefore, a second opinion on Cash's checked swing was not sought.

Had the 1–1 pitch been ruled a strike, however, Cash would have struck out on the dandy curve he took from Gibson on the next pitch. He would not have lasted long enough to start the rally he did—the rally that decided the game. Following Cash, Willie Horton bounced a single to left on the first pitch thrown to him. It was his first hit in three games against Gibson. With Cash advancing, it was the first glimpse of second base we'd had all day.

However, that didn't mean we were about to cash in against Gibson with Jim Northrup at the plate. In his two previous at-bats, Northrup had taken a third strike and popped out to third. In three games of facing Gibson, he was 1-for-9 against him, so Northrup hadn't exactly figured him out yet.

But maybe it was a good omen that Northrup had accounted for our only run off Gibson in Game 4 with a fourth-inning home run. And in our Game 6 blowout, he demonstrated his power again with a grand slam off Larry Jaster. Those home runs were hit in situations that paled in importance to this one, however. As intense a player as you'll ever see, Northrup suddenly was in the spotlight. And he knew full well the potential impact of the moment. We all did.

He was hitting with runners at first and second with two outs in the top of the seventh inning of a scoreless Game 7.

Northrup tugged at his belt, then readjusted his batting helmet as he got ready to face Gibson. McCarver, meanwhile, went to the mound for a discussion while the tension grew. "We're not afraid of him," Northrup had said after Gibson's dominating performance in Game 1. "I'm anxious for the next time."

Well, here it was—the next time after the next time. And he made the most of it.

On the first pitch, Northrup hit a deep slicing drive to center that Flood butchered from the start. He took a step in and then stumbled while trying to correct his mistake. By the time he recovered, the ball was far over his head. "I don't want to make any alibis," Flood said later. "I misjudged it. I started in on it and didn't pick it up out of the background until I knew it was over my head. Then I slipped. It was my fault."

Off to the races, Northrup ended up with a two-run triple. For years the argument has raged about whether Flood would have caught the ball had he not made any mistakes. Always one to defend the purity of the hit, Northrup would become incensed at such a suggestion. "The guys on the bench all said he wouldn't have gotten there in time," Northrup used to say. To his dying day, he felt he had hit the ball so hard that Flood didn't have a chance to catch it.

I personally have always thought it was way over his head, no matter what. Plus it was slicing away.

But to us at the moment, the only important thing was that we suddenly led 2–0 against the great Gibson. And we'd gone from laying off his pitches or flat-out missing them to hitting them solidly. When Freehan followed Northrup's triple with a double to left-center, our lead climbed to 3–0. Man, our dugout was a happy place. But we hadn't won it yet. We couldn't start thinking we had. It was after we scored those three runs that I went up to Mayo, tapped him on the shoulder, and said, "Now I'll finish it for you."

I had struck out to end the top of the seventh, but there'd been no intention of using a pinch-hitter for me. Gates Brown never even went to get his bat. It was clearly my responsibility to bring it home for us.

Going into the bottom of the seventh, I was pretty pumped up. When I struck out Orlando Cepeda to begin the inning, I was throwing harder than I had been earlier. The lead solidified my approach. No nibbling, I went after 'em. I could taste it. But we had an outfield mix-up of our own that we had to get past first.

Following Cepeda's strikeout, Shannon's fly ball to left-center was a ball that should have been caught. Northrup and Horton both went for it, but it glanced off Northrup's glove for an error. McCarver, who already had walked and singled off me in Game 7 and was hitting .360 in the series, was the next batter. I probably don't need to say it was a welcome out when he hit a high, harmless fly ball to Kaline in right. Maris then ended the inning with a pop-up to Stanley at short. There were six St. Louis outs to go.

Gibson bounced back from the three runs he allowed in the seventh to retire the side in quick order in the eighth. We were still being aggressive at the plate, but with Gibson needing only four pitches to get three outs, I didn't get much rest between innings—not even an entire cigarette's worth.

Right back to the mound I went.

With one out in the bottom of the eighth, the Cardinals let Gibson bat for himself. They had used a pinch-hitter, Phil Gagliano, who grounded out to third for the first out, to bat for their hitless shortstop, Maxvill. But with no power on the St. Louis bench—and also as a tribute to how well he had pitched—Gibson was given the chance to help himself offensively. I struck him out.

That brought up the troublemaker Brock, whom I walked on four pitches. They weren't four intentional balls. The 2–0 pitch should have been called a strike in my opinion, but once again our tormentor was on base. Mayo came out to the mound at that point to remind me that we led by three runs, so not to be overly concerned with Brock. To be honest, I don't remember exactly what he said. But I know what he didn't say. He didn't ask me how I felt. That's because I had an understanding with managers my entire career not to ask me how I was feeling. They knew I would always give them the answer most likely to keep me in the game. It was better for them to ask my catcher, usually Freehan, how I was doing. I wanted Bill to be honest, though. I never would have held it against him if he had told Mayo: "Mickey's running out of gas." But he didn't. Thankfully.

In any case, with Brock running on the pitch, Julian Javier surprisingly tried to bunt his way on, but he hit the ball firmly to Don Wert at third for the final out of the eighth. Now there were three St. Louis outs to go. But we had one more chance to stretch our lead if we could. Even if we didn't score, the top of the ninth would hopefully last awhile for us. I needed a breather.

It didn't look like it would last long. Cash flied out to right on the first pitch. Proving to be a tough out, Horton singled but also on the first pitch. At that point Gibson had thrown only six pitches to the last five batters he had faced. Fast at-bats are fine, though, if they are productive. So we didn't mind that on the first pitch with two outs, Wert singled to drive in pinch-runner Dick Tracewski from third to give us a 4–0 lead.

If I could taste victory in the seventh, which I said I could, I could literally feel it now. But I still couldn't start thinking we were home free. I had to keep pitching with the calm approach that had served me so well. The hitters due up in the ninth for the Cardinals were Flood, Cepeda, and Shannon. All of them were threats. Flood was the only hitter who'd gotten two hits off me in Game 7. Cepeda had hit a two-run home run off me in the first inning of Game 5, and Shannon was always a dangerous fastball hitter.

I had my work cut out for me. But I kept thinking more positively than that. Thank you, Johnny Sain. Instead of the trouble I could encounter, I focused on my advantages. The Cardinals had scored just one run since the first inning of Game 5, and I had blanked them for the last 16 innings. But you need to be the most careful when it feels like you are in control. Speaking of which, even now when I think of going into that ninth inning, one of my thoughts—because I walked three that day—is this: *I wish my control had been better.* I kept thinking,

Throw strikes, Mickey. Make them hit the ball. I didn't want to help the Cardinals by walking anyone. Yet, as I made my way to the mound, I knew—I just knew—I had won the game.

On a 1–2 count, Flood lined out to Ray Oyler at short. Oyler was our regular shortstop but couldn't hit a lick. So we only used him and switched Stanley to center when we had a late lead. Northrup moved from center to left, taking over for Horton. Despite how well Stanley had played at shortstop the entire series, having Oyler back at short and Stanley in center was our strongest defensive lineup. Cepeda fouled out to Freehan near the screen for the second out.

Wanting it to be a memorable moment, it was then that I began to plan what I would do if the third out occurred on a ground ball or fly ball—something that didn't involve me, in other words. I decided I would drop to my knees with my arms outstretched, look up at the sky, and say "Yes!"

Proud of what I was about to accomplish, coming back on two days' rest to pitch my third complete-game victory of the World Series, my plan was in place. But I had to put it on temporary hold when Shannon hit a two-out home run to cut our lead to three runs. Following the congratulations he received, as Shannon went down his dugout steps, I noticed he started to unbutton his shirt before disappearing into the clubhouse tunnel. He wasn't acting confident that the game would last much longer.

And it didn't.

I have had a lot of people over the years tell me they'll never forget Caray saying, "McCarver pops up" when the

Cardinals' catcher followed Shannon by swinging at the first pitch I threw to him. To them, it was an iconic moment. To me, it was as well.

Freehan camped under the pop-up in foul territory between home and first as I shouted his name. Cash was close to the play, maybe too close, so that's why I kept yelling, "Bill, Bill, Bill." We needed no mix-ups. In his book, *Behind the Mask*, Freehan wrote, "All I could think was: 'You've had a bad World Series, now don't drop this one, dummy.'"

Cash backed off. We held our breath…ballgame. When Bill caught McCarver's pop-up, I jumped into his arms. We'd done it, by God. We had won the World Series.

It was 4:06 PM. There was joy in Tigertown.

Chapter 17

Celebrity Status

"Mickey has a lot of guts."

—catcher Bill Freehan

By my count Bill Freehan carried me 10 steps after I jumped into his arms following the final out. For the life of me, I don't know how he did it. If I had weighed only 185 pounds, as the Tigers media guide said I did, it might not have been so bad. But at 215 pounds-plus—maybe even 215-plus-plus—I was no light load. Being the passenger, though, was better than being the carrier. I don't know how far I could have carried Bill— maybe two or three steps. He was a pretty solid guy.

There were some fans who rushed out of the stands to join us celebrating on the field. But it was nothing like it would have been in Detroit if the game had been played there instead of St. Louis. From what I could see, none of the players got hassled, and none of the fans got in anyone's way. They were just happy like we were.

What has changed, though, in the way teams celebrate between then and now is that we didn't stay on the field nearly as long as today's players do. We hugged each other, of course, but championship hats are immediately passed out nowadays when a team wins the World Series. Interviews are conducted all over the place. They stay out there for what seems like an hour. We were gone in five minutes. In another change, which I think is for the better, families are allowed on the field as part of the party. Everything was off limits for families back in the day except for the room or hallway where they were told to gather. *I mean, how festive is that?* Some of us found a way to smuggle champagne and plastic glasses out to our wives, though. Gee, who could I be talking about?

Players today also wear goggles to protect their eyes from whatever gets sprayed. That's smart, but it makes them look like they're from outer space. And sheets of plastic are draped over the lockers to protect the contents from getting drenched. That's smart, too. The plastic sheets aren't always used the way they are meant to be, though. During a Tigers celebration in Oakland one year, I heard that several of the star players used the plastic as a slip-and-slide on the floor. I don't say that critically. I bet it was fun. We probably would have done the same thing. It must have been a manager's nightmare, though. "Don't tell me what they're doing, okay? Just don't tell me," I've been told manager Jim Leyland said when he heard about the mischief that was taking place. Knowing it required his intervention, Leyland quickly left his office to make sure no one was in the process of getting hurt.

Unlike the year in which he joined his celebrating players by moonwalking in Minneapolis, Leyland did not go for a slip or a slide in Oakland. But I do think managers should also have their share of fun while celebrating. Mayo sure did. No one was covered with more shaving cream than he was. In addition to goggles and such, what also contributes to celebrations now is the fact that clubhouses are much larger than they were in older ballparks. They're huge, in fact. At Tiger Stadium, for instance, we never had the room to toss our traveling secretary, Charlie Creedon, into the air on a blanket while shouting "MVP, MVP." But I hear that's how a recent Tigers team honored traveling secretary Bill Brown a few years ago. Heck, the position isn't even called "traveling secretary" anymore. It's the "director of team travel."

The visitors' clubhouse in St. Louis wasn't fancy. We couldn't even think of dunking our owner, John Fetzer, in the whirlpool after Game 7 because the tank was too small. Besides, once for Fetzer was probably enough. We had dunked him at home after we won the American League pennant.

There also wasn't the number of media watching the celebration that there would be now. Don't get me wrong: there were a lot of reporters and photographers milling around our clubhouse in 1968 because, well, there were more newspapers than there are now. Plus, the Detroit newspapers were back from a long strike and appeared to be going all out on their coverage. But because there was no cable television yet, there weren't as many production crews—just those from the local network stations. ESPN was more than a decade away from existing. It was not only a different time to play baseball, but it was also a different time to cover baseball. But because we didn't know anything different, the mob scene seemed huge to us. After all, the Super Bowl was in its infancy, so the World Series was still the biggest sports media event of the year.

Ernie Harwell conducted the postgame interviews on a small stage in the middle of the clubhouse. When he asked Mayo what he thought was the turning point of the World Series, Mayo said it was when we came from behind to take the lead in the seventh inning of Game 5, the rally that my one-out single triggered. We had trailed until then because of the home run I allowed to Orlando Cepeda in the first inning. In his postgame comments, though, I appreciated it when Mayo said, "Mickey did a good job of keeping us in it."

About Game 7, Freehan said he'd been worried about me in the middle innings. He felt I might be getting a little tired but added that I "just kept fighting and fighting and fighting. Mickey has a lot of guts." Those words meant a lot to me.

My uniform was soaking wet as I stepped up to speak with Ernie. When he shook my right hand, I easily transferred the champagne bottle I was holding to my left hand. You could tell from how soaked my shirt was that I'd already been an active participant in the partying.

Picking up on what Freehan said, Ernie wanted to know if I'd gotten tired during the game. I told him, "No, but I felt weak from about the third inning on. I didn't have my real good hard fastball, but I kept making it sink and I got 'em out."

The Most Valuable Player award was presented by *Sport* magazine. When I was told I'd won it, I thought to myself, *Great, I'll get the Corvette.* But General Motors wasn't the sponsor that year. Dodge was. So I won a Dodge Charger GT.

Nothing against Chargers, nothing at all. It's just that I already had two of them in my driveway. Oh well, it was a huge honor to be named MVP all the same. I've always been immensely proud of that award. I even told George Cantor for his book, *The Tigers of '68,* that the World Series changed everything for me. Because it did. "It wasn't only about getting recognition," I said. "It was like I turned over a new leaf in my mind. I finally knew I was a good pitcher."

For years after the World Series, though, Bob Gibson wouldn't speak to me. We'd see each other at the Equitable Old-Timers Games in which we played, but he never said a word to me—kind or otherwise. Then one day we were at County Stadium in Milwaukee, waiting to be allowed into the clubhouse so we could get ready to play in the Old-Timers Game. There'd been some kind of screw-up about our arrival, so before the festivities began, we were all standing around in the concourse—American and National Leaguers together. Somebody asked me, while I was waiting, how I felt about Bob Gibson. "How do I feel about Gibson?" I replied, not knowing he was behind me. "My God, what a great pitcher. He had one hell of a World Series against us. I respect that man from top to bottom. I have no ill feelings against him whatsoever."

At that point I felt a tap on my shoulder. I turned around, and there was Gibson. He shook my hand, said, "Thank you, Mickey," and we've been friends ever since.

In fact, we've been such good friends that years ago I was at a signing session with Bob in St. Louis. His line was way out the door. In my line there was no one. I don't mean almost no one. I mean literally no one. "I'll tell you why," Gibson said to me. "To the people in this city, 1968 doesn't exist. They've wiped it out of their memories." He then turned to the crowd and said with a loud voice, "Hey, everybody, we have a World Series MVP here! Get his autograph."

People started getting in my line after that and even chatting with me...but only because the truly great Bob Gibson told them to.

My Better Half...In Her Own Words

Mickey was a superstitious eater, that's for sure. If he pitched a good game after having a particular meal, you knew he would want the same thing the next time he pitched. But if he pitched badly, he'd never want that kind of sandwich again.

I was an American Airlines flight attendant, though I still say "stewardess." Mickey was new to Detroit. I was new to Detroit and I had always loved baseball, though my favorite player wasn't a Tiger. It was Willie Mays.

We got married in 1964, bought ourselves a house north of Detroit soon after, and still live there. He was from Oregon; I was from Hollywood, Florida, but even after his years with the

Tigers, we felt that Michigan was a great place to raise our kids. We never left.

Mickey and I are opposites in many respects. For instance, he slept like a baby before all his starts in the World Series. But I didn't. Before the game, during the game, I worried about everything. I had a habit of rolling my ticket with my fingers when he was pitching. Back and forth, I rolled it, back and forth. I didn't even know I was doing it. I wish I hadn't done it, though, because those tickets would have been great keepsakes. But by the end of each game, they were pretty worn out. So was I.

Mickey is the calm one. It's nothing for him to stay cool. Me? I'm excitable and noisy. I have to admit: more than once I've told fans to shut up if I thought they were getting on my husband too much. I didn't attend all the Tigers home games, but I rarely missed Mickey's starts. I probably made what would be considered a lot of noise. It helped to relieve the stress of the game.

When it came to the World Series, though, it wasn't as easy to do so because I was one of only two Tigers wives to whom the Cardinals gave bad seats. It was just the luck of the draw that the two of us—Jan Hiller, John's wife, was the other one—were out by the bullpen far away from everything. Well, because we were so far away, I took out my movie camera in the second game and was panning around the ballpark when Jan suddenly exclaimed, "Joyce, he just hit a home run. Mickey just hit a home run!"

My immediate reaction was to say, "What?" I'd never seen him hit a home run. To the best of my knowledge, he never had hit one. But here I was, shooting ballpark scenes while he was into his home-run trot. I never got it on camera, but I did see him go back and step on first base to make sure he had touched it.

I'm one who believes that things happen for a reason, though. If I had seen him actually hit the home run, I probably would have made a spectacle of myself out there among Cardinals fans. As it was, Jan and I were the only ones standing and cheering. That's why I always liked the comfort of the wives' section. You could yell for the Tigers all you wanted there.

By 1968 we'd had a daughter, Kimberly Ann, who sat with me during the World Series. It didn't help much when it turned out that we were behind a post for Game 5 at Tiger Stadium. Again, the luck of the draw. One of those lovely "obstructed view" seats at the old ballpark, remember? The ones where you had to lean left or right to fully see what was going on. I can't remember to what side I was leaning when Lou Brock was called out at the plate in the crucial fifth-inning play that changed the momentum of the series. I could see, but it wasn't easy. It also meant that I probably didn't have a good look at Mickey's one-out single in the seventh inning when manager Mayo Smith kept him in Game 5 instead of pinch-hitting for him with the Tigers down by a run.

We were close to being eliminated. I was a wreck, an absolute wreck. Plus, I was pregnant again and didn't know it yet. Everybody was aware that we had to win that game, but I could tell that the long anthem had disrupted Mickey's routine. He had started the game without being ready. We were behind, but it got noisy in the wives' section again when Mickey's single in the seventh led to another by Dick McAuliffe—and eventually to the rally that not only decided Game 5, but also made a comeback against the Cardinals seem possible.

It was after that game that one of Mickey's uncles carried Kimberly down to field level so she could give her daddy a big kiss. It turned out to be a front-page photo. Having Kim at the game was fun because we wore matching blue-and-white outfits. But I knew that Mickey would be too busy to look for us, which proved correct. "I didn't have the slightest idea where you were sitting," he said.

The victory meant the series would return to St. Louis, where the Tigers forced a seventh game by easily winning Game 6. With Mickey starting Game 7, it was essential for me to have better seats than being out near the bullpen. I don't know how she did it, but Sharon McLain made sure all the Tigers' wives sat together for the final game. But even in the wives' section, I was so fidgety. So at one point, I had to go to the bathroom. Several of us did. Lo and behold, that's when we started scoring. There we were, saying, "What's happening? Oh my God, we have to get back to our seats." That completed my unlucky hat trick: I had bad seats for Game 2, sat behind a post for Game 5, and was in the bathroom when Jim Northrup hit his famous triple in Game 7. But I saw the final out and remember saying, "My God, we won. *We won!*" We screamed, we cried…there was a lot of hugging going on.

We weren't allowed in the clubhouse after the game, but Mickey came out to give me a kiss, a hug, and a bottle of champagne. He also handed me some plastic cups so I could share the bubbly. He was looking out for me. But Mickey's idea of looking out for me wasn't always what you would call textbook consideration.

I was overdue with our first child, and his idea of helping at one point was to offer me a ride on the back of his motorcycle. "That might get you started," he told me. Then when I had the baby, he had to leave within the hour for a 10-day trip. There was no paternity leave allowed in baseball back then. I remember him saying, "She's beautiful. Sorry, gotta go." That was hard.

But through all the baseball years followed by the challenge of the doughnut business, our marriage has endured. I kept the books for the shop and did the hiring and firing. He made the doughnuts; I made the muffins. If that's not teamwork, what is?

—Joyce Lolich

Start Your Engines

Here's something I never told the Tigers. I'm pretty sure they would not have liked it.

As the 1968 World Series' Most Valuable Player, I made several appearances as part of a tour I did on behalf of Dodge automobiles for *Look* magazine, which was one of the biggest magazines of its day. The concept was that they would take pictures of us as an active family traveling across the country. We started in California, went to Oak Creek Canyon in Arizona, and then traveled to New Orleans, where we were photographed fishing on Lake Pontchartrain. It was a little shaky that day because the lake was rough, but they got the shots they needed. Actually, the feature was part of a contest, in which there would be a drawing at the end to select the winner of a Dodge Charger from among those who correctly sent in our itinerary on an entry blank. The spread turned out to be two pages. They did a nice job with it.

We were in a different location every day. We flew from place to place, having fun with the sponsors' merchandise—whether it was Coleman camping equipment or on a boat. One of the stops took us to Daytona Beach for a sunrise shoot. After that shoot we were done for the day, so the Dodge people drove us over to the Daytona Raceway, where we met Bill France Sr. and his son, Bill France Jr., the people who ran the place. Dodge was very involved in racing back then, and their people were showing us around when Bill Sr. asked me if I would like to take a spin around the track. Bill, of course, was hugely important in racing. He built Daytona into a famous venue and he co-founded and was the CEO of NASCAR. So when he asked about driving around the track, I knew we already had permission to do so. Not having to be asked twice, I said, "Sure, that would be great."

"Well, we have a Dodge Charger over here that we will use," he said.

It was a car I was familiar with because I already had two Chargers when I won a third for being named MVP. The Charger they had at the track was a full-blown race car but with all the passenger seats still in it because they used it for specialized rides like the one I was going to take. Bill Sr. said my family could come along if they wanted, which they did. We'd gone around the track twice when Bill Sr. said, "Drive into the pits." Buddy Baker was a well-known driver back then, and we were using his pit.

My family got out of the car while Bill Sr. was talking to the pit crew. We thought our time on the track was over. But all of a sudden, the crew started adjusting the car's tire pressure. "Okay, let's go!" Bill Sr. exclaimed. And I got back in behind the wheel without my family. I pulled out of the pit and was coming out of Turn 2 when he said, "Position yourself in the center lane and take your speed to 125 miles an hour."

That was above the limit. They didn't allow anyone except NASCAR drivers to go faster than 100 miles an hour on the track. So I was already up to where the Tigers wouldn't have liked it. The man himself, Bill France Sr., was telling me to take it up to 125 miles an hour, though, and being a car guy, I was fine with it. I didn't mind driving fast. Besides, what the Tigers didn't know wouldn't hurt them. But we were only getting started. Heading into the banking in the center lane at that speed, Bill Sr. said, "Take your hands off the wheel." *Take my hands off the wheel?* What a crazy thing to say.

What I didn't know was that at 125 miles an hour and with the centrifugal force involved, the car would follow the center lane all around the track without my guidance. "That was fun," I said.

"Do it again," Bill Sr. responded.

So I did. I didn't have to steer at all. Because of the banking, the speed, and the combination of both, the car would follow its line—as if it had a mind of its own. Just picture the look on Tigers general manager Jim Campbell's face if I'd told him, "Look, Jim, no hands at 125 miles an hour."

So as we're coming out of Turn 4, Bill Sr. told me to go into the pits, and again I thought we were done. But again I was wrong. "Jack up the pressure!" Bill Sr. ordered the pit crew. So that's what they did. When I heard him say, "Okay, let's go," I pulled out. "Turn it loose," he told me.

I knew that 125 mph was safe, but all caution was about to be thrown to the wind. When I came out of Turn 2, I punched it. The speedometer down the straightaway read 180. I backed off for the turns and then pushed it again for the straightaways and ended up doing four laps. When we returned to the pits, Bill Jr. came running up, yelling, "Jesus Christ, Dad, what the hell are you doing? You can't have Mickey driving that fast around the track. If something had happened, he could have been hurt, and the Tigers would have sued us. The headline would have been all over national news that, 'World Series MVP Mickey Lolich hits wall at Daytona.'"

"But he didn't, did he?" Bill Sr. replied.

I think Bill Sr. had enjoyed the spin around the track as much as I had. Then he turned to me and said, "By the way, your four-lap average was 156 mph. It takes 155 for a driver to qualify for his rookie license. You just qualified. But we aren't going to tell anyone, are we?"

No, we weren't going to tell anyone. And never did. Until now.

My "Career" in Showbiz

If I hadn't been the World Series MVP, several unique opportunities would have been denied me—such as my two-week singing career in Las Vegas. Mickey Lolich and the Four Scores didn't record any No. 1 hits, but we had a lot of fun. And my acting career wouldn't have featured its only movie.

Are you telling me you've never seen *The Incredible Melting Man?* No problem. Few have. I played the sheriff who was killed by, who else, the Melting Man. I had one line. I also was supposed to fire a gun at the monster, but it jammed on the first take, necessitating a second while pissing off the director. I promise you it was a real movie with real ratings. Real low ratings, unfortunately. There were some critics, in fact, who called it one of the 100 worst movies ever made.

My singing career was measured by weeks; my acting career was measured by days—two of them. That's how long I needed to be in Hollywood to shoot the one scene I was in. My agent, Bob Fenton, knew a producer who was looking for extras, so Bob asked if I could be in it. The answer, surprisingly enough, turned out to be yes. "I'll be damned," the producer said, when told the World Series MVP was available. "We have a movie coming up with some bit parts available. Send him on out to us."

The Incredible Melting Man was about an astronaut who had landed on Saturn, where he was infected by a virus causing him to melt. He returned to Earth, needing to consume flesh to stay alive. We filmed the damn thing the winter after the World

Series of 1968, but I've seen a release date of 1977 on it. It probably took them that long to decide whether to release it at all.

My role—despite being labeled "sheriff" in the credits—was as a security guard in a power plant at night. There are fewer scenery costs if you film at night. My partner was supposed to be another Fenton client, Charlie Sanders of the Detroit Lions, but at the last minute, Charlie couldn't make it. They filled in with a local actor instead.

As a security guard, I was on patrol at the power plant when all of a sudden I saw some goo on the floor. To add to the suspense, there was even more goo on some steps leading up to a platform, so, of course, we started climbing. At the top of the steps, sure enough, there was the Melting Man. And my big line was: "Stop or I'll fire. Who the hell are you?"

I pulled out my .38 loaded with blanks and was supposed to fire six shots at him, but the gun did not go off. "Cut, cut, cut!" The director said.

I opened up the gun and was looking at the chamber inside when some guy came running up to me yelling, "Don't touch that gun, don't touch that gun! I'm the firearms expert here."

I handed the gun to him, saying, "You might know something about guns, but this one has a broken firing pin."

Stunned I already knew what was wrong with it, he looked inside and all he could say was, "Yeah, you're right." So they had to get another gun.

This one worked, and while I was firing at the creature as he got closer to us, the picture went to black on purpose. When it did, you could hear a lot screaming as the Melting Man killed me, apparently consuming my flesh. He also consumed my acting career because I never got another call.

The best part of my two days in Hollywood was watching the preparation. When the Melting Man would dress for his scenes, they'd put a mask on him and then pour Karo corn syrup with red dye over him. The worst part is that they used a bucket of it, and the goo would eventually get everywhere. My wife, Joyce, who was an observer on the set, watched it get messier by the minute. At one point she even blurted out, "Yuck!" The actor playing the part then started chasing her, and she ended up running through that power plant as fast as she could. "I didn't want any part of that mess," she said.

My singing career wasn't sloppy like my movie career was, but it was more fun. For one thing, it lasted longer. Plus, I actually had a good singing voice. I sang on *The Joey Bishop Show*, which was a big TV variety show at the time. I subbed at the Roostertail in Detroit for Patti Page for three nights when she got sick. And I spent two weeks singing in the lounge at the Frontier Hotel in Las Vegas as the opening act for Vic Damone. I also sang solo for 10 days at the Detroit Auto Show.

So let the record show that I did have some musical ability. I'd been in the glee club and choir in high school and had put together a quartet. But it came out of the blue when the Frontier called, wanting me as an opening act. Not even Fenton knew I could sing. I'd been rehearsing with a group called The Four Scores. It was a gimmick act with instruments that included a toilet seat made into an electric guitar. The guy who played it called it a "gui-toilet."

The important thing is that the Frontier liked the concept. We joined whatever unions we needed to join in order to perform and onto the stage in Vegas we went. After two weeks, though—and just when we thought we were headed into a third week—they pulled the plug on us, saying it was sort of my fault. It wasn't about the job we were doing. That had nothing to do with it. They liked us well enough to extend the contract, but we weren't spending enough money in the casino after we performed. So the booking agent told us we were done. He said performers in Vegas were expected to head to the casino after their shows. What they paid the entertainers, in other words, they usually got back.

We weren't big enough gamblers for them. I'd take a $20 bill to play blackjack. If I won $20, I'd walk away. If I lost $20, I'd also walk away. The guys in the band had been looking forward to a third week, but they said, "If you don't want to piss away the profits, Mick, we don't blame you." At the end of the two weeks, I was able to cover Joyce's losses at the nickel slots with what I won at blackjack. Big spenders we weren't—and never would be.

It was cool to see our names up on the Frontier's marquee—"1968 World Series MVP Mickey Lolich and the Four Scores"—but I never considered myself much of an enter-tainer, except for my ability to throw baseballs and duck line drives. I knew some songs but not many of them. Tennessee

Ernie Ford's "16 Tons" was one of my favorites. After getting paid for what I did in Vegas, though, and after taking care of all the people I had to pay, I had enough money left to buy a cottage on Hubbard Lake in northern Michigan. So we came out ahead.

Those gigs after the World Series—just that one winter—marked the beginning and also the end of my professional singing career. I never sang again. Except in the shower.

Chapter 18

The Year After

"I hated to leave Detroit."

—pitching coach Johnny Sain

I've heard it said—even by some of my former teammates—that we should have won again after 1968. In fact, Willie Horton has been outspoken about it. In the book *The Big 50: Detroit Tigers*, Willie said, "I wish [manager] Mayo Smith had been harder on us the year after we won. We got off to a good start, then relaxed. With a Billy Martin-type, we would have won. I still get mad thinking we didn't win more with the team we had."

There's no denying we still had talent. We won 90 games in 1969. That's the mark of a good team—but not necessarily of a championship team. With one winning streak after another, the Baltimore Orioles won 108 games. They ran away from all the other teams in the division. By June 28, for instance, they were in front by 10 games and never led by fewer than that the rest of the way.

Several of us had better seasons in '69 than in '68. Denny McLain was among those who did not, but it would have been unrealistic to think he could win 31 games again. With a 24–9 record and a second consecutive Cy Young Award, Denny had an outstanding season all the same.

Jim Northrup had the strangest season among our position players. He improved his batting average from .264 to .295, but his RBI total went down from 90 to 66, so I don't know if he had a season he was happy with or not.

Probably not. Jim was a good friend of mine, but he was a grumbler.

Unlike the relatively calm waters of our championship season, there was a major clash within the ranks in 1969, but it didn't involve players. Not directly, anyway. Our biggest problem was the turmoil that existed between Mayo and pitching coach Johnny Sain. The pitchers really liked Johnny and got along with him, but he didn't like it when Mayo meddled. Then again, Sain hadn't liked interference anywhere. Johnny also didn't like the fact that Mayo began to operate without his input. Johnny was fighting a losing battle, though. Any clash between a manager and a coach is bound to end only one way. The manager will win—and, sure enough, Mayo won.

On August 10, 1969, when Johnny admitted to general manager Jim Campbell that he had gone to the media with his complaints about Mayo, Campbell dismissed him. I was sorry to see it happen. I thought highly of Johnny. He was a positive thinker who helped me a lot, but this was the fourth time in his career he had clashed with a manager. He had to know how it was going to turn out because every job he'd had in the majors ended the same way. In other words, it wasn't long before he was heading home to Arkansas. "I hated to leave Detroit," he told the *Detroit Free Press*. "But Mayo and I didn't see eye to eye on how to run a pitching staff. And, after all, he's the manager."

Sain didn't think Mayo was paying attention to his suggestions. For awhile they had calmly coexisted. Then their working arrangement wore thin. "I couldn't sit on my hands any longer," Johnny said. "I felt I wasn't contributing anything."

Even so, for a defending world championship team to fire its pitching coach less than a full season after winning is a major move—one the Tigers knew was not going to be entirely popular. But the feelings on both sides were strong. For instance, one of the position players on the team said anonymously that he didn't know how Johnny's firing could hurt the pitchers because "only two of them have pitched worth a damn anyway."

George Cantor of the *Free Press* nailed the real problem with this analysis: "Sain saw his pitchers as delicate, sensitive performers who must be understood and protected. Mayo saw them as playing cards, hot-hand tools for a specific function." It might have been the tipping point, however, when Johnny said about Mayo: "Even the most successful business executive can sometimes use a suggestion from his janitor. But my suggestions didn't count for that much here."

After refusing to comment, Mayo finally got tired of Sain's side of the story. "I understand he complained that none of his suggestions were followed," Mayo told reporters. "Well, I don't know to whom he was making those suggestions. They certainly weren't made to me. That was the biggest problem with John. I could never get a straight yes or no answer from him. There were times I just couldn't understand what he was driving at."

As you can see, the situation became too hot for the Tigers to handle. So Campbell let Johnny go. We went on a 15–6 tear for the first three weeks without him, but we only gained one-and-a-half games on the front-running Orioles during that stretch. The Birds were not going to be caught.

September was when we played our worst that season. Before we won four of the last five games, we went 9–17. We held onto second place, but that wasn't consolation compared to what we accomplished in 1968 and to what we had been predicted to do again. "Our final record was 90–72," Bill Freehan wrote in his book *Behind the Mask* in 1970. "I'd predicted at the start of the season we would win the pennant with 98 wins. My prediction, like most of the season, was a disaster."

It was widely written at the end of the '69 season that Mayo would have to crack down on McLain the following year or it would erode our morale. Erode it further was more like it. Cantor wrote, "McLain is a great pitcher. But he isn't above the rules. Or he shouldn't be above the rules. The way things were handled this year, he definitely was."

Several players agreed with that assessment, and they said so in a team meeting that McLain did not attend. Freehan later wrote that Mayo had no idea "of the effect Denny's actions had on the rest of the team." But here's the thing, Bill added it wasn't just Denny—a lot of players took advantage of Mayo.

The net effect is that the doorway to mediocrity had been pried open and wouldn't soon close. We'd win only 79 games in 1970, Mayo's last season as our manager. Despite rebounding in '72 and getting into the playoffs, we wouldn't reach the heights of 1968 again for 16 years. Joy in Tigertown had been fun while it lasted.

Chapter 19

The 1970s

"He is more flamboyant, outspoken, and flashier."
—*Detroit Free Press* columnist Joe Falls

Billy Martin was my favorite manager. Given his reputation for being a hothead and the fact that I wasn't one, that might come as a surprise to you, but he was my favorite because he was fair. Whether it was good news or bad, he always let you know where you stood. He didn't make you guess. I was all over the map with managers in my career, both in the majors and minors. I played for guys I liked a lot, some I sort of liked, and a few I didn't like at all.

My opinion of them never depended on how skilled a decision-maker they were in the dugout. Or whether we had a good team while they managed us. To me, it was a matter of who was up front with the players, who kept his word— compared to someone else who maybe told you one thing and then did another. Billy was hired after the 1970 season, Mayo Smith's last. There was no way Mayo was going to survive the horrible second half we had that year. We went from being nine games over .500 at the All-Star break to having a 32–45 record following the break. As the media often pointed out, we fell apart.

By the end of the season, Mayo had decided he didn't want to be back. Two years after we'd won the World Series with him at the helm, he was fed up with a lot of things, including some of the players and a lot of the fans. Heavily booed throughout his last year for many of his moves, Mayo insisted he wasn't bitter when he left, but you could have fooled me. It sure sounded like he was. "This is a great sports town," he told the *Detroit Free Press* after his final game, "but let me tell you one thing: the baseball fans in this city are ignorant. They couldn't tell a ballplayer from a Japanese aviator, and that's a quote. They'd rather see you stick with a pitcher who's had a good game but might lose it because he's getting tired rather than call in someone fresh from the bullpen who might win it."

The transition had long since begun, though. At the end of the 1970 season, Billy was already in place to be our next manager. *Free Press* columnist Joe Falls wrote: "Martin will have one great edge when he takes over. Because he is more flamboyant, outspoken, and flashier than the man he is succeeding, he will have a natural appeal to the players on the Tigers."

Billy cemented that so-called advantage by meeting with us individually as soon as he could. I liked that approach, liked it a lot. Each of us who lived in or around Detroit was invited to come downtown for a discussion that winter. When it was my turn, I met him for lunch. At that meeting Billy said, "As far as

I'm concerned, Mickey, you're the best pitcher on the team. I will tell you right now that the first seven innings of a ballgame belong to you, no matter what the score is."

He later reduced the number of innings to six, but the message remained clear. Whatever trouble I got into before the seventh, I'd have to get out of myself because my manager wasn't going to bring anybody in from the bullpen. I remember skeptically wondering how soon that comment would be tested. Well, the first time I got into early trouble, I looked into the dugout at Billy, and there he was. His arms were folded, and he didn't move. I figured it was up to me to get out of the fix I was in. When the inning was over and I got to the dugout, he said to me, "What in the hell were you looking at?"

"I was looking at you," I replied. "Things weren't going so well out there."

"Do you remember what I told you?" he shot back with liberal use of his favorite profanities. "You're in there for six innings, no matter what. If you get into trouble, it's up to you to fucking figure it out."

That was Billy for you. But it worked with me. That first year under him I made 45 starts, won 25 games, and threw 29 complete games. I never had to worry about being taken out early. And I have to say, it was a great feeling. What he said filled me with so much confidence that I had a hell of a year in 1971—followed by another in 1972.

Granted, he may have given the same speech to others, saying they were the best pitcher he had—like Joe Coleman, who won 20 games in '71 and 23 in '73—but it didn't bother me if he did. I liked Billy. But there were players who hated him. Jim Northrup despised him. There were others who felt the same way. Martin didn't care if he was liked or not, however. He cared about managing as he saw fit.

On the first day of spring training in 1971, Billy said there were going to be 14 bread-and-butter players on the team: eight position players, four starting pitchers, and two relievers. "They're going to be the guys I turn to all the time," he said. "You other 11 guys, whoever you turn out to be, I want you to keep your fucking mouth shut. If I hear any of you guys pissing and moaning that you're not playing, you're going straight down to Triple A. I might eventually call on you, and if you do well, you might begin to play more. But in the meantime, damn it, I'll have no whining."

Blunt as always, he got his message across point blank. And the guys, for the most part, responded well to him. We had a good year in 1971. Northrup, of course, always wanted to play more center field than he did, but Mickey Stanley still deserved to play a lot because he was such a good athlete. So Northup didn't play all the time—and he didn't like that.

Billy, it turned out, had some flexibility in his plans. Most of the at-bats that season were shared by nine players, not eight. But only three—Bill Freehan behind the plate, Eddie Brinkman at short, and Aurelio Rodriguez at third—played in more than 140 games. Other than myself, Coleman, and Les Cain, however, no Tigers pitcher started more than 15 games. Fred Scherman and Tom Timmerman were the busiest relief pitchers. Instead of the 8–4–2 alignment Billy had talked about, it was more like 9–3–2. But there was a lot less complaining than the year before and much more focus on winning, which paid off with a 91–71 second-place record, an improvement of 12 wins.

We weren't close to the division-winning Baltimore Orioles at the end. We finished 12 games out, but there's no denying that Martin got the best out of a bunch that looked just the year before like it was fading fast. In short, we were heading in the right direction again.

My New Pitch

As it had previously, fate intervened on my behalf in the spring of 1971. Just when I needed a new pitch, I found one. The cutter.

Johnny Sain had tried to teach it to me when he was the Tigers' pitching coach. No matter how hard he worked with me, though, I couldn't master it. To throw it I needed to be confident in it, which I wasn't. Sain would call me a rock head for not being able to throw it. He would also tell me it wasn't that hard. But I just wasn't getting it. I had to feel it and I wasn't feeling it.

Coming out of the 1970 season, I didn't think I was done as a pitcher, but it was far from my best year and far from my favorite finish. In my last 13 starts of 1970, I went 4–7 with a 4.93 ERA. My numbers were a warning to me. Results like that couldn't continue, and the key to improvement was on the outside corner against right-handed hitters. I had to be able to hit that corner.

With my sinking fastball, I'd always been anywhere from a shin-guard's width off the outside corner of the plate—to the corner itself. I had learned to consistently hit that location during a game. It was close enough to be tempting but couldn't be reached by a right-handed hitter if thrown correctly. Many a frustrated opponent would walk away from the plate muttering about it. Suddenly, though, I found myself wandering too far off the plate with my sinker—even farther than I'd been. Hitters were laying off it. For nearly a decade, it had been my bread and butter, but now I couldn't throw it where I wanted.

Then out of the blue, while experimenting with a grip, I said to myself, *Let's see what happens if I give it a little kick with my index finger. Maybe I'll be able to move the ball over.*

The next pitch hit the corner. So did the one after that. I remember thinking, *That's interesting. Let's see if I can do it again.* So I gave it the same kick, and it did the exact same thing. I kept throwing it, as if I had found gold. By then, I was thinking, *Damn, that's the pitch Sain tried to teach me for three years. I finally learned it—and Sain's not here.*

In 1971 he was with the Chicago White Sox. We were in Lakeland, Florida, at spring training when I first experimented with the cutter. But I didn't say anything to anyone right away. Then I took the new pitch into an exhibition game and still hadn't mentioned it. I couldn't wait to see the reaction.

So there I was picking up my target as usual, just outside the corner, as if nothing had changed. I threw the sinking fastball that Gerry Staley had taught me in 1962, and the ball headed for the outside shin guard. Like it always did. *Okay, there's my sinking fastball, blah, blah, blah,* I said to myself. *Same old, same old.* I pitched one inning with my usual stuff. But in the second inning when Bill Freehan called for a sinker—and me being a smart ass—I threw a cutter instead.

The pitch was dropping toward the shin guard again, and then, all of a sudden, the sucker moved over six to eight inches, and I cut the black of the plate on the outside corner. There it was—my new pitch. Well, Freehan quickly called time and walked out to the mound. "What the hell was *that*?" he said.

"Why do you ask?" I replied.

"What a great pitch," he answered, "my God, that was fantastic."

I told him I was trying to learn a cut fastball, to which he said, "Learn? You got it. But I'd sort of like to know when it's coming. We need a sign for it."

"Let's use three fingers down," I said.

"Done," Freehan replied.

From that point on, one finger was for the sinker, two was for the curve, and three was for the cutter. It changed our sign system, but far more than that, it changed me as a pitcher.

To me, the cutter was the easiest pitch in the world to throw. All I had to do was change the pressure alongside the ball a little bit, putting a football spin on it with no strain on my arm whatsoever. Really, it was as natural as can be.

It reduced my walks and my pitch counts. But by lowering my counts, it added innings for me. I threw 100 more innings in 1971 (376) than I did in 1970 (272). That was the start of four years in a row in which I threw more than 300 innings.

I'm as proud of that achievement as I am of anything I ever did in baseball. Yes, I was a guy who'd had a good World Series in 1968 and I was tremendously proud of being the series MVP that year. I still am. But the cutter came along at a time when I really needed it—in my ninth year of being a major league pitcher. Without a doubt it extended my career.

I didn't show it much to American League teams that spring, but I couldn't wait to trot it out against the White Sox so that Sain could see it for the first time. After I had thrown it, he walked over to me later and said, "You finally learned how to throw the fucking cutter, didn't you?"

"I sure did," I replied.

It was a fun pitch to throw. Right-handed hitters would think it was going to be six inches outside, so they often took it. Then, bang, I'd drop it on the black. If they looked back to question the call, the umpire would simply say, "It hit the corner."

Seriously, it changed me. I became a different kind of pitcher when I added the cutter. I've never been a big stats guy, but right-handed hitters dropped from a .339 on-base percentage in 1970 to .297 against me in 1971. My strikeout-to-walk ratio climbed from 1.76 to 3.09. And I whittled down the .268 batting average for right-handers against me in 1970 to .240 in two years. All because of the cutter. I won 47 games in 1971–72 combined, along with finishing second in the Cy Young voting in 1971 and third in 1972. I was also an All-Star both years.

I've said that the cutter allowed me to "throw forever," and sometimes it seemed like I did. I faced 1,538 batters in 1971.

No one faces that many anymore or even comes close. Rick Porcello of the Boston Red Sox led the majors in 2017 with 885 batters faced. Times have certainly changed.

The cutter wouldn't break until it was two feet from the plate. By then, unless he was swinging from his ass, the hitter had made up his mind to swing or not to swing. I liked it when a batter would take a step toward first base, thinking it was ball four—only to have the umpire ring them up instead. Many of the guys I faced would come up to me years later and tell me how hard it was to hit "that slider." Slider, cutter, I didn't care what they called it. I only cared that it worked.

The 1972 Season

My three favorite seasons were 1968, '71, and '72 for reasons easily explained. We won the World Series in 1968. I re-invented myself as a pitcher in 1971 with the addition of a cutter. I also earned a save in the All-Star Game at Tiger Stadium that year despite allowing a home run to Roberto Clemente, who was playing in his last All-Star Game as it tragically turned out.

And I put 1972 on the list because it sometimes gets forgotten but doesn't deserve to be. It's only natural, however, that seasons in which you only come close aren't stored in the same golden memory bank as championships. The glow doesn't shine quite as brightly as when you win.

But 1972 was one heck of a year for the Detroit Tigers. Personally, it wasn't too shabby either. In my first 26 starts of that season, for instance, I went 18–6. I had never before won

18 games by the end of July. And with 15 starts remaining, I thought I had a chance of matching the 25 games I won the previous season. But I'd long since become familiar with the twists and turns a season can take. Despite a 2.82 ERA, I went only 4–8 in my last 15 starts to finish at 22–14.

One other personal highlight, by the way, took place in the All-Star Game. I worked two scoreless innings of a close contest the American League eventually lost 4–3 in Atlanta. But in my first inning, I faced three legends and retired them all. Willie Mays took a called third strike. Hank Aaron flied out to right—as did Willie Stargell. What a thrill it was to face (and retire) all three.

Eventually, though, the year's entire focus came down to the pennant race. The season had started late because of a work stoppage over pension and arbitration issues, and the games missed were not made up. That's not the way they would do it now, but it's the way they did it then, creating the possibility of contending teams playing an unequal number of games. As we came down the stretch against the Boston Red Sox, it became evident we weren't going to play the same number.

Much of the '68 team was still together, but I think we knew we were looking at a last hurrah. We didn't know how far we'd get with what we still had, but it was a fun run, I can tell you that. After leading the division for much of the season, we started slipping. By September 11, we were in fourth place, two games out. Suddenly, it felt like 1967 all over again. This time the contenders were us, the Red Sox, the Baltimore Orioles, and the New York Yankees.

A five-game winning streak lifted us into first place. But a 4–5 stretch dropped us back into second. We were bouncing all over the place. With six games remaining, we trailed the Red Sox by one-and-a-half games, but by then at least it was apparent that one of us was going to win the division. The other two teams, the Orioles and Yankees, had either dropped out of contention or would soon do so.

Heading into the final series, we had played one more game than the Sox, and that wasn't going to change because our last three games were against each other at Tiger Stadium. It was possible that one of us might win the division by a half game. A 4–1 victory in the series opener put us back in front by exactly that half-game margin. In one of my best starts, I struck out 15. But it was Woodie Fryman's masterpiece the next day in a 3–1 victory that clinched the division for us. A meaningless loss in the final game meant we finished a half game in front of the Red Sox. The unequal number of games proved significant after all.

No matter how we got there, though, we were in the playoffs with a chance to go to the World Series. All we had to do was get past the mighty Oakland A's, whose lineup featured Reggie Jackson, whose starting rotation featured Catfish Hunter, and whose bullpen featured Rollie Fingers. All of them were future Hall of Famers. It was going to be a tough task. We had to be at our best. And even that might not be enough.

Catfish and I were the starters in the opener of the American League Championship Series at the Oakland Coliseum. He lasted until the ninth inning; I lasted until the 11th inning. But with a 2–1 lead after Al Kaline's home run put us in front in the top of the 11th, I allowed consecutive singles to Sal Bando and Mike Epstein to start the bottom of the inning. I could have kicked myself for Bando's hit. Going into that at-bat, he was 5-for-44 in his career against me. As I described my performance that day, "I had pretty good stuff, but my fastball wasn't popping."

We ended up losing the game when Kaline's throw from right hit Gene Tenace on the hip as he was advancing from first to third on a single off Chuck Seelbach. Tenace scored the winning run on the error. I was the losing pitcher. Losing the opener was a disappointment, but the ALCS was far from over. "We've been known to bounce back from games like this," I said.

We lost Game 2 also but won the next two. I went nine innings without a decision in Game 4 but was reminded of the tenacity that helped make us strong that year. When the A's scored twice in the top of the 10th to take a 3–1 lead at Tiger Stadium, I wondered what I was going to do at home the next day. We were on the brink of elimination from the best-of-five series. Mowing the lawn would have to wait, however, because we scored three runs in the bottom of the 10th to force a fifth game.

It was a series known for an ugly incident. Bert Campaneris, the A's leadoff hitter and sparkplug, heaved his bat at our Lerrin LaGrow in Game 2 after the right-hander drilled him on the ankle with a pitch. Manager Billy Martin had to be restrained from going after Campy, who was suspended for the rest of the series—as was LaGrow. "It was the dirtiest thing I've ever seen in baseball," Martin told reporters. "He could have killed my man. Campaneris is as gutless as any player who ever put on a uniform. It was like using a gun and running away."

But the ALCS that year should also be remembered for its excellent pitching on both sides. The A's just pitched a little better than we did. We lost the finale 2–1. The difference was Jackson's steal of home, a play on which he tore his left hamstring and missed the World Series because of it, in the second inning. The other two runs—one for each team—were unearned.

Fryman started the finale for us. A Kentucky tobacco farmer, Woodie had gone 10–3 after being picked up off waivers from the Philadelphia Phillies in early August. We wouldn't have been in the playoffs without him. Not only did he go 7–1 after September 1, he won the division-clinching game against the Boston Red Sox. The guy was a godsend. I mean, he'd been 4–10 with the Phillies before we picked him up. But he had lost Game 2 to Blue Moon Odom, who blanked us on three hits, and was hooked up in another duel with Odom (followed by Vida Blue) in Game 5.

Fryman didn't give up any hits in the top of the second, but he allowed a costly run. Jackson walked and then stole second. Bando's fly ball to right moved him to third. Epstein was then hit on the wrist by a pitch up and in before Tenace struck out. That's when A's manager Dick Williams made the biggest and most daring decision of the entire series. He called for a delayed double steal. With a 0–1 count on Dick Green, Epstein drew a throw from Bill Freehan by taking off for second. Jackson beat second baseman Tony Taylor's throw back to home plate for

Oakland's first run. Tearing his hamstring on the slide, however, Reggie sobbed on the A's bench after being taken out of the game. "I wanted to play so badly," he said.

Jackson's run only tied the game. A hotly disputed call at first base in the fourth led to the run that beat us, though. Umpire John Rice ruled that Dick McAuliffe's throw from shortstop to first base pulled Norm Cash's foot off the bag. That runner, George Hendrick, later scored on a two-out single by Tenace. Our first-base coach Frank Howard was still so incensed that when he took his position for the bottom of the fourth he was ejected for telling Rice what he thought of the call. "Baseball has been played for 150 years, and they never call a guy safe on a play like that," Howard told *The New York Times*.

Cash was furious as well. "I never cheat unless I have to," he said, "and I had no reason to cheat on that play. It was a lousy call. Everyone knows it."

Fans voiced their objections by throwing firecrackers, bottles, and toilet paper on the field as the game neared its disappointing conclusion. "This is chaos," said A's broadcaster Monte Moore. "Everything that can be done to disrupt this tremendous excitement is being done here."

We hadn't answered with enough offense, though, and that's how we lost the game. Martin said it was "an understatement" to call it the most disappointing defeat of his career.

So we never made it back to the World Series with the ol' gang of Kaline, Freehan, Cash, McAuliffe, Horton, Stanley, Northrup, Hiller, and me. Too bad. We were so close. But we'll always have '68.

Falling Apart

As much as I'd like to, I can't say everything about my career was fun. Most years were, but one definitely was not. The year that wasn't fun was 1975. That's the season we lost 19 games in a row, reflecting the extent to which the bottom dropped out for all of us.

The collapse of '75, however, had its roots in '74. That's the year our World Series team finally began to disband. It was Al Kaline's last season. On the brink of turning 40, Al could still play, but he felt his skills were diminishing. He was too proud to continue his career that way—and rightly so. Norm Cash was released, and Jim Northrup was traded to the Montreal Expos the same day in August. Norm had been my teammate for 12 years; Jim had been my fellow Tiger for 11. Gates Brown wasn't the productive pinch-hitter he'd been for so many seasons. His career was winding down. Of his last four years, only one was respectable. His final season would be 1975.

The core of the 1968 team, which also had reached the 1972 playoffs, was disintegrating. You could see it on the field. But it didn't complete the process until the second half of the '75 season. Man, we fell apart at that point. Through our first 101 games, there was no sign of the complete collapse about to occur. It hadn't been a great season for us by any means in the first four months, but we weren't flat-out terrible. In fact, we put together a solid 18–9 streak in July that lifted us to within nine games of .500 at 46–55. We weren't contending, but at the time, things were looking up, and it appeared as if the second half was going to be better than the first.

We had struggled at times in the first half, but not like we did during the stretch that completely tore us apart. My record was 10–9 when our 19-game losing streak began. To tell you the truth, I thought I was having a pretty good season. Then the wheels fell off. There's no way to dress it up, so I won't. I kept losing. The team kept losing. From being nine games under on July 29, we took the non-stop express to 46–74 by mid-August. We didn't get blown out in many games. At no time, for instance, did we even allow double-digit runs.

But low-scoring games weren't a consolation. They were still losses. During the 19-game slump, we were outscored 102–46. Ray Bare finally ended it with a two-hit shutout of the California Angels in Anaheim. I started the second game of the skid. I also started its last game. In between I lost two other starts. However, I also kept losing after it ended. I finished the season dropping 13 of my last 15 decisions. When I didn't get any run support, I lost. When I got moderate support, I lost. And even those few times when it looked like the offense had given me enough runs to win, I lost.

It was a nightmare. I don't blame anyone but myself, but the offensive numbers don't lie.

Starting when I was 10–5 with a 3.31 ERA, the Tigers scored nine runs in my next eight starts. I lost all eight, of course. But my ERA through the seventh start of that ugly stretch was an acceptable 3.46. I really wasn't doing that much differently than when things were going well. But in these different times, I was losing all my starts. Going into my final start of the season, my record was 11–18.

I won my last start 5–1, but only because I blanked the Boston Red Sox on three hits after allowing a run in the first inning at Tiger Stadium. The five runs the Tigers scored for me that day equaled the number they had scored in my last eight starts combined. In five of the eight, we were shut out, including in three consecutive games before my final start.

Nothing could salvage the season for us by then. To close it out, we lost 21 of our last 25. As far as the Tigers were concerned, it was the year that soured them on keeping me—or at least soured general manager Jim Campbell—because the following December he traded me to the New York Mets, telling me in no uncertain terms that he didn't want me around anymore.

What he said to me hurt deeply—after I'd been with the team for 13 years and in the organization for 18. It was hard to hear how much the Tigers wanted to get rid of me. But they were in desperate need of offense. As a pitcher who often had been victimized by the lack of runs, I understood their needs. And I also knew they could still get a decent hitter for me, which they did in Rusty Staub.

But I still didn't want to leave Detroit.

My memories of pitching for the Tigers remain positive to this day. They'll always be positive. It was with Detroit that I began my career as a professional pitcher, that I played a major role in winning a World Series, and that I enjoyed my greatest individual success.

Earlier achievements didn't keep 1975 from being agonizing, though. Or from being a disaster.

Farewell

I did not expect to be traded at baseball's winter meetings in 1975, and with the deadline just hours away, it was looking like I wouldn't be. But I soon found out otherwise. When Jim Campbell, the Tigers' general manager, called me that night in December, he said he had a chance to make a deal with the New York Mets for Rusty Staub. "But I can't trade you," Campbell said, "unless you okay it because you are a 10-year veteran."

I told him he could take the trade and shove it. Then I hung up on him. No way was I going to the Mets. About three minutes later, Campbell called me back, saying, "Mick, I need to talk to you about this."

"Jim, I have no interest whatsoever in going to New York," I replied. "I never liked New York. When I went there as a player, I lived in the hotel and went to the ballpark. Then I came back to the hotel. That's all I did. I didn't wander around. I didn't do anything. To me, it was just a mass of humanity. Plus I didn't like the attitude there and the way they treated players from other teams at Yankee Stadium."

I knew the deal involved the Mets—not the Yankees—but I figured the things I disliked about New York would be the same. I spelled it out to him again that I didn't want to go. I also said that was my final word. Then I hung up the phone. Pretty soon I got a third call. It was Campbell, telling me I was going to hear from the president of the Mets (J. Donald Grant), to which I firmly replied, "I don't really care, Jim, I'm not going!"

Well, I did get a call from Grant, who said the club wanted me to come to New York and that they wanted to make this deal. He also said I'd make $125,000 a year as a Met in 1976–77 on a two-year contract (after making $100,000 as a Tiger in 1975). I told him politely, "I appreciate the offer, Mr. Grant, but I really don't want to play on your team."

Then Grant must have called Campbell because pretty soon came another call from Jim, and this one had a different tone. "Look, you son of a bitch, if you don't agree to this trade, I'm cutting your salary 20 percent next year," said Campbell, who was furious now. "That's the contract you're going to get from me. We don't need you on the team anymore. You pitch once every four days, and we're trying to trade for someone who plays every day. We don't need you. You're not winning anymore, and I don't want you on the team."

Don't need you…Don't want you…

Those words stung. My resolve to refuse the trade began to waver, and doing the math in my head to justify my change of heart, the difference between what I would make for the Tigers and what I would make for the Mets made me tell Campbell I would call him back. Remember, this was late at night on the last day of trading. The clock was ticking. So I sat down with my wife, Joyce, and explained everything to her. She was adamantly against it.

She'd been a flight attendant and felt the same way about New York as I did. She then said that if I got traded she would not join me nor bring the children to New York to live. She would only bring them for long homestands. Joyce always came to the games I started at Tiger Stadium, but she would not come to my games at Shea Stadium. So there was considerable personal pressure about it. I'd make more money but see my family less. In my mind, though, the fact that the Tigers didn't want me anymore had also become a big factor.

Acknowledging now that I made a mistake, I talked to Campbell again. "Okay, Jim, if that's what you want to do, I'll go to the Mets." I didn't want to, but I went. I pitched there one year without my family. I had absolutely nothing against the Mets as a team. There were some great guys there. Tom Seaver was a great person to be around. I'd heard stories about him being ornery and mean, but he was a great teammate. Jerry Koosman was a joy to be around, too, along with Jon Matlack. There were a lot of guys there—like Joe Torre and Ed Kranepool—that I really liked.

But at the end of the year, I kind of looked in the mirror, and the reality staring back at me was that I was at the downside of my career. Things weren't going so smoothly on the mound for me anymore. That's when you think, *You used to be a good pitcher. Now you're sort of mediocre. Why don't you retire?*

So I retired. I was done. I sat out all of 1977, which made me a free agent the following offseason. But I had no intention of pitching again. Then out of the blue, the San Diego Padres called me, asking if I could still throw strikes. Stunned at their interest, I told them I could. So they invited me to spring training in Yuma, Arizona, in 1978 to try and make the team. I reminded them that I'd been out a year and that my velocity might be down. I knew it could be a little tough, but they offered me a two-year contract for more than the Mets were going to pay me, had I stayed. With that in mind, I had to at least give it a try.

Well, sure enough, I made the team and won the Opening Day game in relief for the Padres against the Giants in San Francisco. But the team's orthopedic doctor noticed that something didn't look right. "Let me check your knee out," he said.

It turned out that a problem, which had been diagnosed a few years back in Detroit as a strained tendon, was actually torn cartilage in my right knee. By that time I'd had the condition for five years, so he operated on it, and I missed half the season. I didn't come back until around the All-Star Game. After that I pitched in relief here and there during the second half of the '78 season and made a couple of starts, but I knew I was done. I went to the front office following the season and told the guys in charge, "Look, I have a two-year contract here, but my days are over. I can't really throw anymore. I've lost velocity."

They reminded me about our "special agreement." In other words, they pretty much told me, "You're coming back, Mickey, whether you want to or not." What was our special agreement? The Padres had three left-handers—Randy Jones, Bob Shirley, and Bob Owchinko—I was supposed to mentor that final year.

To varying degrees they overcame their problems, but after two years of pitching for the Padres and trying to help their young lefties, that was it for me. I'd done my best.

At that point I retired. And this time—at age 39—I stayed retired.

Campbell was still Campbell, though. Stingy and stubborn, he would change later toward Joyce and me, but he hadn't yet. For instance, he set aside World Series tickets for us in 1984 that we paid for. But they were two of the worst seats imaginable. They were almost up to the roof in the second deck at Tiger Stadium. Television crews wanted to come up to speak to me because it was the first Tigers game I'd attended since my playing days. But the steps were so steep that the crews were hesitant to carry the cameras that far. They didn't want to slip. But the good thing was that on a cold night, it was quite warm up there in the ballpark's nose-bleed section.

Campbell and I didn't talk to each other for years after that. Then one day when we both were in Lakeland, Florida—where he had a condo and I was helping out at fantasy camp—my phone rang. "Mickey, this is Jim Campbell. What are you doing for dinner?"

I recognized his voice before he even got his name out. I told him I had no plans, but why was he asking? "Because I'd like to take you and Joyce out tonight," he said.

We were stunned, but we agreed to go. The evening went well. All the angry words that had passed between us when the Tigers traded me were put aside. I'd been heartbroken by that deal, but this was a chance to mend fences. "I appreciate that you and Joyce are longtime friends of mine," Campbell told us at dinner, "and I wanted to be with friends today on my birthday. I didn't want to dine alone."

On the drive back from Jim's place to where we were staying, Joyce told me, "It's time to forgive and forget." She was right. Bygones were finally bygones.

Chapter 20

Doughnut Man

"Yeah, let's do it."

—Mickey Lolich

I frittered away the years after I played baseball. You could even say I apple frittered them away. When I retired from pitching, I bought a doughnut shop north of Detroit and turned it into a family business. I doubt any other ballplayer has ever made *that* transition—from the diamond to doughnuts. But I did. Doughnuts became my job; the bakery became my office: making them, selling them, chatting with the customers as they ate 'em. It was not just a passing fancy. I was in the doughnut business for 18 years. That's longer than I was a major league pitcher.

The year I didn't pitch for the Mets—I call it that because I had a two-year contract with New York but elected to retire after the first season—I got a job in Detroit in specialty advertising, which included logos on golf balls, names of companies on promotional calendars, engraved wristwatches. I didn't enjoy it much but felt it might lead to something else.

It indirectly did. During that year of being away from the game (1977), I often stopped for a cup of coffee and an apple fritter on the way to work. I'd sit in the back room of the shop talking to the owner, who was an avid fan. He had coached with Bill Freehan in Little League, so we shared the common ground of being involved with baseball, though obviously at different levels. Anyway, if I hadn't retired for a year, I wouldn't have met him.

My baseball career wasn't quite over, though. Knowing I could throw strikes in my sleep, I went back to the big leagues to pitch for the San Diego Padres in 1978–79. But then I was done.

Well, my friend who I used to talk baseball with at his doughnut shop called when I was in my final year with the Padres to say another shop was up for sale. He knew it well because he not only had built it, but he also had owned it for 10 years.

He knew it so well, in fact, that he got me interested in it. The couple he sold it to the first time wanted out because they were hoping to open a restaurant elsewhere. They were short of money, so my friend advised me that we should look into buying the shop together. I liked the sound of the arrangement. It was an existing business with an established customer base and at the time I didn't have plans for what I would do in retirement. So I said, "Yeah, let's do it," and we put the money down to buy the R&D Donut Shop.

I remember the Padres were in Cincinnati when I told my wife to write a check for half the down payment. Despite some questions, which I answered the best I could, she wrote it, and that's how we ended up in the doughnut business. I really enjoyed my new line of work because the shop was a great place for people, especially your regulars, to gather and gab.

The partnership didn't last long, though, only about a year and a half. My partner—the former owner and avid Tigers fan, whose name I'd rather not mention—had his own bookkeeper, but my wife, Joyce, wanted a role in the business. That didn't sit well with him. He didn't like women "interfering." "I'm not a partner with *her*," he would say.

"But I am," I'd reply.

It got worse after that. My wife would ask questions at our weekly business meetings, which was fine with me, but it pissed off my partner enough to call her a bad word. That did it. I pushed him up against the wall, telling him never to say that to my wife again. Then I told him our arrangement was over. In only its second year, my time in the doughnut business was about to end with him abruptly announcing his plans to buy me out.

I beat him to the punch, though. I bought him out instead. And all of a sudden, I owned a doughnut shop. Heck, I barely knew the difference between a fried cake and a French cruller.

I'd always been out front in the shop talking to customers while my partner had been the one in back taking care of production. Out of necessity, I became a good student. It took me only two weeks to learn how to make all the varieties.

Besides, I liked doughnuts. My favorite was the old-fashioned with chocolate frosting.

But that's what I had to watch out for—consuming too many of them. I started gaining weight. At one point after I'd brought home a dozen doughnuts every day for a month, my oldest daughter Kimberly said, "Dad, can you buy a Dairy Queen instead? We're tired of doughnuts."

After I bought out my partner, I changed the name from R&D to the Mickey Lolich Donut Shop. I took over the shop in 1981 and did well initially, but we lost our lease in 1983 after thinking we'd have no problem being renewed. That disappointed us, but I found a nice piece of property in Lake Orion, farther north of Detroit. The location was great, but it was five times larger than we needed. I didn't know what was going to happen at that point. But like a lot of what's happened in my life, fate was kind.

The owner of the Lake Orion property came down to talk to us one day while I was busy in the back room of the shop we were closing. "I'm working on the doughnuts," I called out to him. "But if you want to come back and talk, it's fine with me."

I was making doughnuts; Joyce was filling them. As I remember, she had some butter cream on her nose she didn't see. But we were working as a team. Later, we went up the street to a restaurant to speak with the Lake Orion property owner, and it was during that conversation that he said, "I'm a firm believer in working your own business. I've done that all my life. I've had tons of people come to me about that property, wanting to build a fast-food place on it. If I had sold it to them,

I knew someone would buy it, but someone else would run it. I didn't want that. When I came to the back room there at your shop and saw you rolling out the dough, and your wife busy with the filling, I said, 'Now, there's a family working together.'"

Then he asked a question that floored us: "How big of a building do you want? I'll build it for you. I won't sell you the property, but I'll give you a sweetheart lease."

He built us a shop where we did three times the volume we had done at the first location. Man, were we busy. I'll never forget Paczki Day, for instance. I made the genuine Polish paczkis—not the imitations you see in grocery stores. But to stock enough of them by Fat Tuesday, I had to start making them on Sunday. I probably made 120 dozen of them every year. I stayed in the doughnut business until 1997 and sold it then because I received an unsolicited offer, which was too good to turn down.

From pitches to Paczkis—with only a few glitches along the way—I was fortunate to follow one successful career with another. But it never would have happened without those apple fritters.

Acknowledgments

I enjoyed my career. I loved playing the game. So I'm taking this opportunity to thank all the Detroit Tigers who played defense behind me and also did their best to provide whatever offensive support they could—which was enough for me to win more than 200 games. At one of our reunions, I told my former teammates those same sentiments. Plus, I also told them this because I believe it: pitchers don't win games; teams do.

But above all, I thank my family for putting up with my baseball career and all the time I spent away from them. I'm thanking my wife, Joyce, and my three daughters, Kimberly, Stacy, and Jody—plus my extended Lolich family in Portland, Oregon, where I grew up.

Like anyone who played baseball—or has to travel because of baseball—I missed birthdays. I also missed a lot of school events because you can't be in two places at once—and I was probably in Baltimore, Cleveland, or Kansas City when my kids were in plays, concerts, or something else I wanted to attend. That was just a fact of life.

But it wasn't a fact of life for my grandchildren—Michael, Justin, Ryan, and Danny. I was retired by the time they were born. I've been home for their birthdays. They never saw me play, though. So I wanted them to know my story. Through this book, my grandchildren and children will now know more about me than they've ever known. They'll know how I became what I became.

—Mickey Lolich

"When the Bengals bring the pennant home..." It was the song of the season—our anthem of 1968. Some of us still sing it. The Tigers did indeed bring the pennant home that year. Then they won a great World Series. And now, 50 years later, I had the honor of writing a book with one of the heroes.

Only nine pitchers in history—Mickey Lolich and eight others—can accurately make the five following claims.

Among all-time major league strikeout leaders, he's in the top 20.

He threw more than 190 complete games.

He threw more than 40 shutouts.

He started more than 495 games.

He won more than 215 games.

But only one of the nine can add a sixth statement to the first five: he accomplished it all in only 16 seasons. Only one of the nine can add a seventh statement to the first six: he was the Most Valuable Player in a World Series. Only one of the nine can add an eighth statement to the first seven: he pitched three complete-game victories in the same World Series. And only one can add a ninth true statement to the first eight: he's not a Hall of Famer. Never even came close.

Lolich, who ranks 19th among strikeout leaders and fourth among left-handers with 2,832 innings, is the one pitcher who can make all nine statements if he were so inclined.

Not bitter about the lack of recognition, though, this is what Lolich says about his own career:

"I did okay."

Yes, you did, Mickey, to say the least. To write this book with Lolich has been a privilege. It's also been a pleasure getting to know him.

I'm not sure it would have happened had it not been for a friend of mine, Bill Dow, suggesting that I consider such a project. Bill has done quality work for many years as a freelance feature writer in Detroit. He laid the foundation for Mickey to realize his dream of writing a book by conducting a series of interviews with him for a comprehensive story that appeared in *Baseball Digest*.

Bill permitted me to use those taped conversations as an informational source, sparing Mickey the burden of going over some of the same ground twice. It is with gratitude that I credit Bill for his assistance.

It is also with gratitude that I acknowledge the conscientious editing of Triumph's Jeff Fedotin and my friend, Dan Marowski.

I spent 38 years covering the Detroit Tigers as a beat writer—all but two of those traveling for *The Detroit News*. On a daily basis, I covered two of the four pitchers I would put on the Tigers' Mount Rushmore of starters—Jack Morris and Justin Verlander.

I clashed with the combustible Morris at times. I didn't clash with Verlander. But in the end, I knew Morris better. Both were highly competitive, of course. Their drive to be the best is part of what made them successful. Occasionally, when he fell short, Morris would take his disappointment out on the media by being difficult to get along with.

Verlander didn't have such a personality trait. There weren't as many layers to him as there were to Morris. Even if there had been, he didn't wear them as publicly as Jack did. But Morris, quite frankly, was easier to read. He wore his emotions on his sleeve. His trouble with the media was the result of nothing more than a compulsion to be as competitive with us as he was with all his perceived opponents. As Jack got older, though, he mellowed. He made himself easier to like.

Another pitcher on the Tigers' Mount Rushmore is Hall of Famer Hal Newhouser, whom I never saw pitch and with whom I had too few conversations. The longest talk I ever had with "Prince Hal" lasted two-and-a-half hours on a flight from Detroit to Miami for the winter meetings. He was a scout for the Houston Astros at the time. I was so fascinated with his memories that predated my earliest awareness of baseball that I wished we could have had many more discussions, but we never did.

When this project began, Mickey was the only one of the four I didn't know at all. Once, when he was subbing on a Tigers broadcast, I shared a cab with him in New York, heading to the team hotel in Manhattan. It was a pleasant enough conversation, but nothing I expected him to remember me by. I could have been just another newspaperman, but Lolich was always different that way. He is different in a lot of ways, he likes to say, but making an honest effort to get along with reporters was certainly one of them.

Even without knowing him, I always thought that Lolich was "underwritten about." He'd been a chapter in several books but never the central focus of one. As was sometimes the case during his career, he was overshadowed by more flamboyant teammates—nothing against Denny McLain, but he certainly was one of them. In retirement, Lolich—other than the attention he received for owning a doughnut shop—faded as a Tigers personality.

Then the years started passing quickly. He was pigeonholed with a reputation for being capable but not colorful, which, it turns out, was not fair. I mean, I've now known only one player who, instead of shagging flies during batting practice on a day he wasn't scheduled to pitch, unscrewed the light bulbs of the ground-level auxiliary scoreboard at Tiger Stadium as a prank. Little could Lolich know—but he could always hope—that his foil, general manager Jim Campbell, would completely take the bait and urgently call for an electrician, only to be eventually told that someone had played a trick on him. To this day you can imagine the blustery Campbell—somewhat resembling *Dennis the Menace*'s Mr. Wilson—huffing, puffing, and saying, "You son of a bitch" when he discovered the prankster was Lolich.

Mickey missed the great paydays of baseball, topping out at $125,000 in multiple seasons, but if you adjust the sum of his salaries for inflation, he earned less than $5 million in his career. A pitcher with a $20 million salary in today's game earns that in less than two months. It again underscores the different era in which Lolich played.

But more than any reason why the pitchers of his day deserve respect is the workload they took for granted. While it's true that Lolich averaged 330 innings a season for the four consecutive years (1971–74), in which he redefined the term "horse," he also faced 5,408 batters, an amazing amount for a four-year stretch. The 1,538 batters he faced in 1971 alone still ranks as the most for any pitcher in the majors since 1923. By either measure Lolich pitched as much in four years as an ace now faces in six. That's how much the game has changed.

But returning to my original premise, the other eight pitchers on the list who featured a historic combination of strikeouts, wins, shutouts, starts, and complete games are Nolan Ryan, Steve Carlton, Bert Blyleven, Tom Seaver, Gaylord Perry, Phil Niekro, Ferguson Jenkins, and Walter Johnson.

Bob Gibson and Cy Young came close to making the list, but Lolich started more games than Gibson and ranks two spots higher than Young on the list of strikeouts. Many others fell by the wayside because no one pitches complete games or an abundance of shutouts anymore. Given the parameters, Mickey is in pretty good company, wouldn't you say? What's more, it's not a list that is going to grow. Those days are long gone.

My favorite moments of doing the work required to write this book were the days I spent with Mickey as he recovered from back surgery and got ready for knee surgery, watching YouTube replays of the three games he won in the 1968 World Series. He said it was the first time he'd seen them since he started those games.

There was a look on Lolich's face as each game neared its conclusion that convinced me he was completely enthralled by what he was watching. Finally I understood why. *My God*, I said to myself, *in his mind he's back on the mound.*

So here's to No. 29 for the pitcher he was. You, sir, had one hell of a career.

—**Tom Gage**

Bibliography

Wire Services
Associated Press

Periodicals
Baseball Digest
Detroit Free Press
The Detroit News
The New York Times
The Sporting News

Websites
baseball-almanac.com
baseball-reference.com
blessyouboys.com
detroitathletic.com
mlive.com
sabr.org

Writers
Jack Berry
George Cantor
Bill Dow
Joe Falls
Jerry Green
Jim Hawkins
Dan Holmes
Jeff Samoray
Charlie Vincent
Pete Waldmeir

Video
A City on Fire: The Story of the '68 Tigers, HBO Sports (2002)

Books

Cantor, George. *The Tigers of '68—Baseball's Last Real Champions*. Taylor Publishing Company (1997)

Freehan, Bill. *Behind the Mask—An Inside Baseball Diary*. The World Publishing Company (1970)

Gage, Tom. *The Big 50 Detroit Tigers—The Men and Moments That Made the Detroit Tigers*. Triumph Books (2017)

Green, Jerry. *Year of the Tiger*, Coward-McCann, Inc. (1969)

Wendel, Tim. *Summer of '68*. Da Capo Press (2012).